English Life in the Eighteenth Century

English Life in the Eighteenth Century

Roger Hart

"Far from the madding crowd's ignoble strife,
Their sober wishes never learn'd to stray;
Along the cool sequester'd vale of life
They kept the noiseless tenor of their way."
Thomas Gray (1716–77) *Elegy Written in a
Country Churchyard.*

WAYLAND PUBLISHERS LONDON

THE ENGLISH LIFE SERIES

English Life in the Seventeenth Century
English Life in the Eighteenth Century
English Life in the Nineteenth Century

Roger Hart

Copyright © 1970 by Roger Hart
First published 1970 by
Wayland (Publishers) Ltd
101 Grays Inn Road London WC1
SBN 85340 002 4

Printed in Great Britain by Jarrold & Sons Ltd, Norwich

Contents

PREFACE

Many excellent books have been written about particular aspects of eighteenth-century England, especially in the fields of political, economic and cultural history. In this volume, however, the author has had a different objective – to try to capture something of the daily life of the ordinary English family at that time, unaware as they generally were of the broader sweep of events. In preparing this account, extensive use has been made of contemporary material, in order as far as possible to let the people of two centuries ago speak for themselves. We are fortunate in having many extremely lively spokesmen – not only Englishmen like Dr. Johnson, Daniel Defoe and Arthur Young, but foreign visitors like C. P. Moritz and César de Saussure.

For the first time, perhaps, the Englishman had consciously begun to think of himself as a civilized, "genteel" character, whose firmly based institutions seemed to make any return to the social and religious barbarities of the past quite unthinkable. Ordinary people enjoyed a far better standard of living than ever before, and with the opening up of road communications felt optimistic about achieving a better and more humane society. Perhaps this, more than anything else, accounts for the ebullience of the age.

R.W.H.

The ballroom: Hogarth's caricature of growing English pretensions to gentility

1 Fashionable Life: London

The Ruling Classes

IN 1700, England and Wales contained about 5,500,000 people, a tenth of the number today; the ruling class consisted of a few hundred families, all acquainted with each other in this small circle, and linked through marriage. These families, such as the Pelhams or the Russells, were great landowners, whose nominees filled the House of Lords and House of Commons. Yet it was not entirely a closed society, certainly not as closed as its continental counterparts. By the 1700s it was beginning to include the new men, whose families had won eminence in trades, speculation or the professions. They included the Pitts, the Beckfords, the Clives, the Childs, the Yorkes and others; William Pitt's grandfather had been a tough diamond-trader; Beckford was a tradesman who rose to become Lord Mayor of London; Clive rose to pre-eminence through his career in India. Although nearly all the members of the ruling classes were very rich, poverty alone never disqualified anyone. Those unfortunate peers who had fallen on hard times, perhaps after the South Sea Bubble, claimed as their right foreign embassies or colonial governorships, or even straight pensions from the Secret Service fund. Lord Hardwicke said, "I look upon such pensions as a kind of obligation upon the Crown for the support of ancient noble families whose peerages happen to continue after their estates are worn out." These families regarded themselves as the rulers of Britain by right.

The activities of the ruling class were varied; many served as Ministers or other officials; others took an active part in commerce, agriculture and, in the later part of the century, industry. They included agricultural improvers, such as Coke of Holkham, and canal builders such as the Duke of Bridgewater. Many, however, took little part in affairs outside their country estates, or in advancing relatives and dependants in posts and sinecures in the administration or armed services. For those inclined to it, the eighteenth century was an age of elegance and leisure; the great country houses of the rich, such as Cliveden or Stowe, were rural paradises, designed by Robert Adam, Inigo Jones or John Nash, filled with art treasures and antiquities from every corner of the globe. Many people remarked on the formal gardens, laid out by such men as Capability Brown, which adorned them. Lord Kinnoul wrote, "The

Above William Beckford, famous as one of the first tradesmen to become Lord Mayor of London. *Below* Inigo Jones

Left Wentworth House, Yorkshire, a stately home showing the new interest in classic architecture. *Right* "Grace before meat, or a Peep at Lord Peter's," a cartoon satirizing the piety of many of the nobility

laying out of the ground in a natural way is carried to greater perfection in England than in any part of Europe. In foreign countries . . . the taste of gardening is forced and unnatural. . . . They constrain and counteract nature."

Robert Adam in 1773 noted "a remarkable improvement in the form, convenience, and relief of apartments." He explained: "The massive entablature, the ponderous compartment ceiling, the tabernacle frame, almost the only species of ornament formerly known in this country, are now universally exploded, and in their place we have adopted a beautiful variety of light [designs], gracefully formed, delicately enriched and arranged with propriety and skill. We have introduced a great diversity of ceilings, friezes and decorated pilasters, and have added grace and beauty to the whole by a mixture of grotesque stucco and painted ornaments together with the painted rainceau with its fanciful figures."

At the start of the century, as in earlier times, manners were atrocious; swearing and obscenities were common, uncouth behaviour taken for granted. During a conversation about swearing between Boswell and General Paoli, "The General said, that all barbarous nations swore from a certain violence of temper, that could not be confined to earth, but was always reaching at the powers above. He said, too, that there was greater variety of swearing, in proportion as there was a greater variety of religious ceremonies." Yet as the years passed, there was more appreciation of social refinement, and in these graceful mansions genteel conduct became the accepted code. Lord Chesterfield wrote to his son (1751), begging him to learn genteel manners from his dancing-master: "Desire him to teach you every genteel attitude, that the human body can be put into; let him make you go in and out of his room frequently, and present yourself to him, as if he were by turns different persons; such as a minister, a lady, superior, an equal, an inferior, etc. Learn to sit genteelly in different companies, to loll genteelly and with good manners in those companies where you are authorized to be free: and to sit up respectfully where the same freedom is not allowable. . . . Take particular care that the motions of your hands and arms be easy and graceful, for the genteelness of a man consists more in them than in anything else, especially in his dancing."

The beau: male fashions became increasingly dandified

8

The leisured classes of the time greatly enjoyed talk and conversation, and included among them many celebrated wits, whose reputation grew in the fashionable *salons* and coffee-houses. Dr. Johnson, however, regretted the passing of real hospitality and entertainment: "In a commercial country, in a busy country, time becomes precious, and therefore hospitality is not so much valued. No doubt there is still room for a certain degree of it; and a man has a satisfaction in seeing his friends eating and drinking around him. But promiscuous hospitality is not the way to gain real influence. You must help some people at table before others; you must ask some people how they like their wine oftener than others . . . being entertained ever so well at a man's table, impresses no lasting regard or esteem."

He added sourly, "No, Sir, the way to make sure of power and influence is by lending money confidentially to your neighbours at a small interest, or, perhaps, at no interest at all, and having their bonds in your possession."

Above Children of the time were dressed as miniature adults

Servants

The smart eighteenth-century footman often identified himself completely with his master, for instance insisting on himself being called "my lord marquis," if his master were a marquis. This snobbery was carried to absurd lengths, for example with the footmen of bishops dressing themselves in purple liveries, and demanding to be addressed as "my lord bishop." It is said that the footmen of Members of Parliament even went so far as to hold their own parliaments.

Footmen's livery was provided by their masters, and probably other clothing as well; footmen also did well out of tips, known as "vails," which were always heavy when the household was entertaining; vails were expected for the smallest service, such as taking a coat. But the footmen needed these benefits; in the early part of the century, their average wage was only about £6 a year, though it later rose to nearer £14. Footmen in country houses, outside London, would not do as well, though they had other compensations such as more spare time and chances for sport. In a great house, with many different ranks of servant, promotion was slow, and people were fiercely jealous of their jobs and privileges.

A big aristocratic house, such as Bedford House of the Russell family in London, would have many servants – not only footmen but maid-servants, cooks, kitchen maids, coachmen, chaisemen, postilions, carpenters, pages, gardeners, and ruling over all a butler, or head housekeeper. Page-boys were not usually paid anything except their board and lodging, though they sometimes received presents, and were taught to read and write or play musical instruments, such as the flageolet. Cooks and kitchen maids were paid about £6 a year, though a top French chef might earn as much as £60. The cost of keeping servants in a great house was very high; Bedford House in 1771 had forty-two indoor and outdoor servants, costing altogether £859. 16s. 0d. a year. Negro slaves, known as "blackamoors" sometimes worked as servants, but they were not common; Dr. Johnson had one called Francis.

Above Famous inn sign showing "The Running Footman"

Servants of a wealthy household giving scraps to singing beggars

Running footmen in the livery
of the Duke of Marlborough

The following advertisement was placed in a London newspaper of the time, by a footman seeking a job: "A likely sober person . . . has a mind to serve a Gentleman as a Valet de Chambre or Buttler . . . he is known to shave well and can make Wigs; he well understands the practice of Surgery which may be of great Use to a Family in the country, or elsewhere . . . he is a Sportsman; he understands Shooting . . . Hunting, and Fishing."

Servants won a special reputation for corruption and rudeness, if we are to believe contemporary accounts. The rowdy ill manners of London footmen at the theatre (see page 67) was proverbial; foreign visitors complained that since servants' wages were so low, it was they – not their hosts – who kept them, with vails. To visit a friend's house for dinner could easily cost ten shillings or a guinea in vails. Many a maidservant saw herself as a great lady, putting on airs; they did not have to wear a uniform: "Her neat's leather shoes are now transformed into laced ones; her yarn stockings are turned into fine white ones; her high wooden pattens are kicked away for leather clogs; she must have a hoop as well as her mistress; her poor scanty linsey-woolsey petticoat is changed into a good silk one, four or five yards wide at the least. In short, plain country Jane is changed into a fine London madam; can drink tea, can take snuff, and can carry herself as high as the rest." (*Eighteenth Century London*, Sir Walter Besant.)

One lady became so angry with one of her maids, that she put this sarcastic notice in the newspaper *Poor Robin's Intelligencer*: "A maidservant to be hired, either weekly, monthly or quarterly for reasonable wages. One that is an incomparable slut, and goes all the day slipshod with her stockings out at heels; an excellent housewife that wastes more of everything than she spends; an egregious scold, that will always have the last word; an everlasting gossip, that tells abroad whatsoever is done in the house; a lazy trollop, that cares not how late she sits up, nor how long she lies in in the morning; and in short, one that is lightfingered, knowing nothing, and yet pretending to know everything."

Mrs. Purefoy, a country lady, described what she expected of her cook-maid: "She must milk 3 or 4 cows & understand how to manage that Dairy, & know how to boyll and roast ffowlls & butchers meatt. Wee wash once a month, she & the washerwoman wash all but the small linnen & next day she & the washerwoman wash the Buck. She helps the other maid wash the rooms when they are done, she makes the Garrett beds & cleans them & cleans ye great stairs & scours all the Irons & scours the Pewter in use, & we have a woman to help when 'tis all done. There is very good time to do all this provided she is a servant, & when she has done her work she sits down to spin." The work was hard indeed. (Note: "buck" meant large quantities of coarse linen.)

Fashionable Shops

Europe had no shops to compare with those of eighteenth-century London. Napoleon implied a compliment when he called the English, "a nation of shopkeepers." Paris had famous shops, but none to compare with the number and opulence of those in London. Dr. Johnson suggested

The milk girl, a common figure
in towns and villages

The signs prominently displayed above shops were the forerunners of advertisement hoardings

to Goldsmith, "Let us take a walk from Charing Cross to Whitechapel, through I suppose the greatest series of shops in the world." Archeholtz, a visitor from Prussia said: "The magnificence of the shops is the most striking thing in London; they sometimes extend without interruption for an English mile. The shop front has large glass windows and a glass door. In these the merchant displays all that is finest and most modern, and as fashion compels him to make considerable changes, the variety and symmetrical arrangement provide for the passers-by the most brilliant *coup d'œil*." He describes the windows of the silversmiths as filled with "prodigious heaps of gold and silver."

The diarist William Cole noted in 1765: ". . . as the Brilliancy & Shew of ours in London make one of its chief Beauties and Ornaments, so the dead gloom of the City of Paris is nothing beholden to its tradesmen in shewing their Goods to the best Advantage. . . ."

The German visitor to London in 1782, C. P. Moritz, noted: "Especially in the Strand, where one shop jostles another and people of very different trades often live in the same house, it is surprising to see how from bottom to top the various houses often display large signboards with painted letters. Everyone who lives and works in the house sports his signboard over the door; indeed, there is not a cobbler whose name and trade is not to be read in large golden characters. . . . I have found 'Dealer in Spirituous Liquors' to be the most frequent inscription among them." Moritz added, "In London, care is taken to show . . . all works of art and industry to the public. Paintings, machines, precious objects – all can be seen advantageously displayed behind great clear glass windows. There is no lack of onlookers standing stock still in the middle of the street here and there to admire some ingenious novelty. Such a street often resembles a well-arranged show-cabinet."

A shopkeeper's best customers were the wealthy upper classes and nobility, who were in the habit of passing "an idle hour" in a shop, for conversation and to meet their friends. It was in a bookshop, for instance,

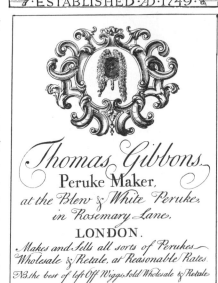

"Bucks" (fashionable young men) shopping at the drapers

Chairmaker's shop in Clerkenwell, London

that the famous meeting between Boswell and Johnson took place. Deard's the "bauble shop," Betty's the St James's fruiterers, and Wedgwood's china shop were others noted for their social atmosphere. Browsing, then as now, was a national pastime, and a draper had to be careful not to show impatience, even if he had to unfold a hundred pieces of material without making a sale; and if a sale were made, he had to offer the best service possible. As a French visitor noted, "If a two-shilling purchase is made he will offer to send it to the other extremity of the town, and if the customer spends several pounds, he is sure to be invited to his table, or at least regaled with a glass of wine, a cup of chocolate or some other refreshment."

R. Campbell in *The London Tradesman* (1747) described the ideal shop assistant: "He ought to speak fluently, though not elegantly, to entertain the ladies: and to be the master of a handsome bow and cringe: should be able to hand a lady to and from her coach politely, without being seiz'd with a palpitation of the heart at the touch of a delicate hand . . ."

Shops flourished in the market towns in those parts of the countryside where the gentry had their country villas and seats. Stamford, where Robert Owen served his apprenticeship to a draper, was a famous shopping place throughout the eighteenth century, and Guildford was another; shops tended to reflect local industries, for example the stocking shops in eighteenth-century Liverpool.

The streets of London

London was growing rapidly and haphazardly – "a head too big for the body." Houses were cramped together, streets were narrow, and darkened by huge signs hanging on ornamental brackets, carriages jostled with pedestrians. C. P. Moritz wrote in 1782, "You will never see a sensible man walking in the middle of the road except when he has to cross over." The bad street manners of the first part of the century improved a good deal, and was noted by foreigners, especially from the violent streets of Paris. Dr. Johnson also noted it: "In the last age, when my mother lived in London, there were two sets of people, those who gave the wall, and those who took it: the peaceable and the quarrelsome. *Now* it is fixed that every man keeps to the right: or, if one is taking the wall, another yields it; and it is never a dispute." But the streets were still dangerous; brawls could easily begin, with people pushed into the gutter; footpads roamed the unlit streets at night, causing someone to write:

> Prepare for death if here at night you roam,
> And sign your will before you sup from home.

Heads of traitors could still be seen sticking on spikes at Temple Bar in 1746 after the Jacobite Rising; a visible violence.

Filth from shops and houses was slopped down the central gutters in the cobbled surfaces. This scandal was a continual cause of concern, and prompted many Paving Acts in Parliament. Many of these failed, although impassioned speeches were made, such as that of Lord Tyrconnel: "The filth, sir, of some parts of the town, and the inequality and ruggedness of others, cannot but in the eyes of foreigners disgrace the nation . . . putrefaction and stench are causes of pestilential distempers . . . the present neglect of cleansing and paving the streets is such as ought not to be borne."

"Nothing in London makes a more detestable sight than the butchers' stalls," wrote Moritz in 1782, "especially in the neighbourhood of the Tower. The guts and other refuse are all thrown on the street and set up an unbearable stink." In theory every man had to remove his own rubbish, and was responsible for repairing the piece of pavement by his front door; but not until the Westminster Act of 1762 were improvements put in hand – paving-stones laid in place of cobbles, large signs laid flat against walls instead of hanging out. Jonas Hanway, the philanthropist, was glad to see all this, for the sake of "an elderly female, stopped in the street on a windy day, under a large old sign loaded with lead and iron in full swing over her head, and perhaps a torrent of rain and dirty water falling near from a projecting spout, ornamented with the mouth and teeth of a dragon . . ."

Every visitor to eighteenth-century London was impressed by the noise and the throng of people. Dr. Douglas wrote in 1749, "Most of the streets in Paris are as little frequented on week days as those of London on Sundays," and in the 1780s, Wenderborn noted that "more people are seen in London at midnight than in many considerable towns of Europe at noonday." Most noise was caused by the ironshod wheels of carts and carriages and the clatter of hooves; for many stage coaches and wagons entered and left the city in the middle of the night; noise was made by bellmen announcing their wares, and by tradesmen shouting, coupled with the noises from taverns, coffee-houses, shops, the riverside, and the main thoroughfares and places of entertainment; the scavenger with his cart rang a bell, as did the collectors of the "penny post."

Last but not least were the street criers who sold their wares by singing traditional verses – always a feature of English town life. There were street cries from ballad-sellers, cherry-sellers, second-hand clothesmen, knife-grinders, coalmen, milkmaids, sellers of watercresses, cat's- and dog's-meat, slippers, doormats, strawberries, chimney-sweeps, match-sellers, rabbit-sellers, apple-sellers, gingerbread-men, chair-menders, oystermongers and many others.

Left Angry words in a crowded street. *Top* "Poor Jack" the street seller. *Above* The chimney-sweep with his boy. *Below* News-vendor selling *The London Gazette*

"Johnson," wrote Boswell, "was much attached to London: he observed that a man stored his mind better there, than anywhere else; and that in remote situations a man's body might be feasted but his *mind* was starved, from want of exercise and competition. No place, he said, cured a man's vanity or arrogance so well as London; for as no man was either great or good *per se*, but as compared with others, he was sure to find in the metropolis many his equals and some his superiors. He observed, that a man in London was in less danger of falling in love indiscreetly, than anywhere else; for there the difficulty of deciding between the conflicting pretensions of a vast variety of *objects*, kept him safe . . . He could not leave the improved society of the capital, or consent to exchange the exhilarating joys and splendid decorations of publick life, for the obscurity, insipidity and uniformity of remote situations."

Above Dr. Samuel Johnson, famous for his wit and love of London. *Below* The coffee-house. *Bottom* A chop-house

Coffee-houses

The coffee-house reached its peak of popularity in the eighteenth century, with about 3,000 in London. Coffee-houses took their character from those who frequented them. There were coffee-houses for rich City merchants, such as Jonathan's, where stocks and shares changed hands every hour in the days before the modern Stock Exchange was built; there were coffee-houses for writers and wits, such as the St. James's, Turk's Head, Bedford, and Peele's, where Dr. Johnson went; there were coffee-houses for sportsmen, such as White's (still flourishing today) and William's. One of the best known of all was Garraways, which later became better known as an auction house.

Ned Ward's book *Secret History of Clubs* gives much fascinating information on coffee-houses of the day. He tells of a visit to Old Man's in Scotland Yard: "The clashing of their snuff-box lids (in opening and shutting) made more noise than their tongues. Bows and cringes of the newest mode were here exchanged . . . they made a humming like so many hornets in a country chimney." C. P. Moritz visited some coffee-houses in 1782 but found them quieter. "In these coffee-houses, quietness is the rule. If they speak, they speak softly together. Most of them read the papers, and nobody disturbs another." But polite conversation did not typify every club; some, like Almack's, were devoted to gambling. Walpole wrote in February 1770 that "the gaming at Almack's is worthy the decline of our empire . . . the young men of the age lose ten, fifteen, twenty thousand pounds in an evening there. Lord Stavordale, not one-and-twenty, lost £11,000 there last Tuesday, but recovered it by one great hand at hazard."

The eighteenth century brought the agricultural revolution, and saw a remarkable growth of the population; overseas trade prospered, science and invention flourished, literacy developed, and communications by road and canal improved. In an age of such activity, the coffee-houses, and other clubs, mug-houses and taverns, played an important role in public affairs, before the great institutions of the nineteenth century had been founded. The coffee-house was club, bank, newspaper library, stock exchange all in one. "The true felicity of human life", said Dr. Johnson, "is in a tavern."

Macaronis and Beaux

Every country and period has had its wild fashions; England has seen "gallants, bloods, bucks, beaux, fribbles, macaronis, fops, monstrosities, corinthians, dandies, exquisites and swells." But in eighteenth-century England, none were so remarkable as the Macaronis. The first Macaronis were a group of fashionable young men, recently returned from the Grand Tour, who formed a small club called the "Macaroni Club," because they always ate a dish of macaroni, then little known in England. They took London by storm: nothing was fashionable that was not *à la macaroni*. Even the clergy began to have their wigs combed *à la macaroni*, their clothes cut *à la macaroni*; there were turf or racing macaronis, clerical macaronis, military macaronis, college macaronis, and many other varieties.

Many people strongly disapproved. One said: "No handsome fellow will belong to them, because their dress is calculated to make the handsome ugly, and the ugly ridiculous. His hat (like his understanding) is very little . . . he has generally an abundant quantity of hair, and well he may, for his shoes are reduced to the shape of slippers, on the surface of which appears a small circle of silver, which (he tells us) is a buckle . . . He is the sworn foe of learning." Here is a description of the complete outfit of a beau, drawn up by a contemporary:

Five fashionable coats full mounted, two plain, one of cut velvet, one trimmed with gold, and another with silver lace
Two frocks, one of white drab with large plate buttons, the other of blue with gold binding
One waistcoat of gold brocade
One waistcoat of blue satin, embroidered with silver
One waistcoat of green silk trimmed with broad figured gold lace
One waistcoat of black silk with fringes
One waistcoat of black cloth
One waistcoat of scarlet
Six pairs of cloth breeches
One pair of black velvet breeches
Twelve pairs of white silk stockings
Twelve pairs of black silk stockings
Twelve pairs of fine cotton stockings

Above "Mademoiselle Parapluie," or "foolishly fashionable." *Below* Fop sporting a frock-coat and club-wig

Left A coffee-house's character depended on its clients. *Below* "Jonathan's" where rich City merchants exchanged shares and gossip

Above The gorgeous clothes of the rich showed up the drabness of most clothing

Above "Tempers fray:" fashions' excesses delighted cartoonists

One hat laced with gold *point d'Espagne*
One hat with silver lace scallopped
One hat with gold binding
One plain hat
Three dozen fine ruffled shirts and neckcloths
One dozen cambric, one dozen silk handkerchiefs
Gold watch with chased case
Two valuable diamond rings
Two mourning swords, one with a silver handle
A diamond stock buckle
Set of stone buckles for the knees and shoes
Pair of silver mounted pistols with rich housings
One gold headed cane
One snuff-box of tortoise-shell mounted with gold

The manners of fops were a byword. In her best-selling novel *Evelina*, Fanny Burney described an invitation to dance: "Bowing almost to the ground, with a sort of swing, and waving his hands with the greatest conceit, after a short and silly pause, he said, 'Madam, may I presume?' and stopt offering to take my hand. I drew it back but could scarce forbear laughing. 'Allow me, Madam,' continued he, affectedly breaking off every half moment, 'the honour and happiness – if I am not so unhappy as to address you too late – to have the happiness and honour–."

Johnson disliked foppery. "It was the bad stamina of the mind, which, like those of the body were never rectified: once a coxcomb, always a coxcomb."

Wigs and wig-makers

The enormous periwigs of Queen Anne's reign soon went out of fashion, to be replaced by smaller wigs. One wig-maker, William Philips, offered a typical variety – public brown bob-wigs, cut or dressed 14*s*; "scratches", also 14*s*; grizzle bag-wigs, 21*s*; grizzle bobs, cut or dressed, 21*s*; dark majors at 18*s*; brown bag-wigs at 15*s*. After 1760, large dress-wigs gave way to the toupee (an array of curls over the forehead and the side of the face, a word which has recently returned to fashion!). Dignity was needed to wear a wig, which denoted a person's wealth or status. The old and middle aged were great wig-wearers. Many people shaved their heads bare, banishing grey hairs and natural baldness; the wig was a great leveller. After the 1740s, fashionable people began to wear their own hair long, bunched and tied, and after 1770 powdered it with blue powder, or red powder from about 1777. Under their wigs, they wore linen or silk skull-caps; wigs were removed for sports, or any other energetic activity such as duelling.

"In a century of wigs, shaven heads and smooth faces," wrote Sir Walter Besant, "the barber plays an important part. He had to be visited every day; his apprentices all day long were engaged in making wigs, dressing and curling wigs, powdering wigs, besides shaving heads and chins and cheeks. He kept the Sunday wigs for his customers' use in a box, as a solicitor now keeps the papers of his client; on Sunday morning he and his boys were up early dressing the wigs for church and carrying

Left On a trip to Paris an Englishman has his wig powdered

them around. On weekdays early in the morning, the 'flying barber' was seen with his jug of hot water, his soap and his 'tackle' hurrying from house to house. Later on in the day, his shop was full of City men, tradesmen especially, who wanted an hour's holiday from the shop for a morning gossip, and very often a morning draught."

Wine and Walnuts, published in 1740, describes some curious and elaborate instruments found in a barber's shop: "Long spiral machines, for frosting the hair, various other powdering puffs, toupees, braids, and wired cushions, braiding pins twelve, yea, fourteen inches long, crisping and other irons of every denomination, and leather rollers for the beaux' curls." Above all, the wig was a sign of modern and civilised society.

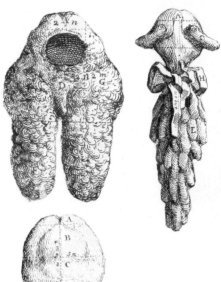

Above A variety of eighteenth-century wig styles

Chippendale London

Although there were many skilled cabinet-makers in London, few specialized in furniture alone, but sold all kinds of merchandise for the comfortable home. The trade card of John Speer, cabinet-maker (1730), reads: "John Speer, Cabinet-maker, etc. at Ye Lion and Lamb, the West side of Fleet Market, sells Leghorn and English Straw, Chip, Horse-hair and all other sorts of Women's Hats, English and Dutch mats, Mahogany, Wallnut-tree and other Chairs . . . with all sorts of Turner's Goods – Wholesale and Retail. Carpenters, Joyners, and Cabinet Work Performed in General." A contemporary of Speer's, Wilson of Aldersgate, advertized himself not only as a cabinet-maker, but "dealer in coals" and seller of "organs, harpsichords, and *piano fortes*."

A fashionable cabinet-maker was often consulted on furnishing a home, being asked not only to make furniture, but to supply household fixtures and fittings, hangings and wallpaper. The Chippendales were one such firm; David Garrick, the actor, put them in sole charge of the decoration of his new house at the Adelphi (designed by Robert and James Adam), and the bill came to £1,000. (Later, Garrick found he could not pay it, and the angry Chippendales had to settle for less.) Argument over bills was very common, and appears to have been an accepted part of business. William Linnell of Berkeley Square, for instance, supplied furnishings to Sir Richard Hoare, who went through Linnell's bill making marks in red ink, "too much" or "extravagant charge." Customers also often took months to pay, or paid in instalments without bothering to ask the tradesman.

Above Street-corner orators were many, their views various

But a fashionable furniture-maker could amass a fortune in eighteenth-century London. One such was Henry Clay who died in 1795 worth £80,000; he accumulated this sum by making the new *papiermâché* furniture (the craft of "japanning") in the fashionable colours of dull blue, black or olive-green, and building up an export business. Thomas Chippendale the Elder was one of the greatest makers of taste, as is shown in his beautiful catalogue, *The Gentlemen and Cabinet Maker's Directory*, published in 1754, intended for "patrons and customers in all classes of society." Hepplewhite and Sheraton were other such leaders of fashion, whose influence was felt far beyond London, and whose advice was sought by the nobility and the rich in designing their homes.

Right The House of Commons as it was seen by people passing through Westminster on the River Thames

Members of Parliament

The eighteenth century saw a great rise in the power of Parliament, and the House of Commons became the dominating power in the constitution. The royal veto was exercised for the last time by Queen Anne in 1707 (on the Scottish Militia Bill). Thereafter, with the Revolution theory of the previous century, the King only acted "officially" on the advice of his Ministers; his Ministers in turn needed the support of Parliament, especially the House of Commons. So it was that control of the House of Commons, patronage and electoral influence became the main concern of the great politicians. The House of Commons member held the key to power.

There were two kinds of Member of Parliament, the County member and the Borough member. The eighty County members were elected on the forty-shilling freehold qualification – that is, by citizens who owned freehold property worth at least forty shillings a year if rented. This was quite a wide part of the population, and led the County members always to claim that they were the best representatives of popular opinion. Yet they usually owed their election to the local support of a powerful and noble family, such as the Pelhams of Sussex, or the Courtenays of Devon, whose grip on local affairs through patronage, wealth, bribes, and family connections was so great, that they could more or less choose the only candidate. If there were two or three candidates at an election, they freely used their influence to bribe and cajole the forty-shilling freeholders, who often owed their living to them, to support "their" candidate. The Duke of Newcastle was the greatest expert in political patronage of his day; his personal influence seemed to reach every corner of English life, north, south, east and west.

The Borough members represented wider interests than the County members; they included lawyers and merchants, contractors, ship-owners, Army and Navy officers, Government officials, East India Company officials and wealthy adventurers who wanted to protect their financial interests. But they did not represent many of the people of Britain. The 204 cities and boroughs in England which elected Members probably only had about 85,000 people. Many seats were managed outright by a wealthy patron, and were known by everyone as "rotten boroughs."

C. P. Moritz visited Parliament in 1782, and did not always approve of what he saw: "Whenever one of them [the Members of Parliament] speaks badly, or the matter of his speech lacks interest for the majority, the noise and laughter are such that the Member can hardly hear his own words . . . I was much shocked by the open abuse which Members of Parliament flung at each other . . . The gist of the debate is often lost in bickering and misunderstanding between each other." But Moritz was much struck by the interest the English people took in politics: "When one sees how the lowliest carter shows an interest in public affairs; how the smallest children enter into the spirit of the nation; how everyone feels himself to be a man and an Englishman – as good as his king and his king's minister – it brings to mind thoughts very different from those we know when we watch the soldiers drilling in Berlin."

Top Sir Robert Walpole in a long career helped establish British democracy by giving effective power to the House of Commons
Centre Charles James Fox, the great Whig famed for his powers of oratory
Left The entrance to the House of Lords, the ancient seat of political power

2 *Life in the Provinces*

Provincial Towns

Here is a table of population about 1770:

Bristol	100,000	Shrewsbury	13,000
Norwich	50,000	Worcester	11,000
Liverpool	35,000	Oxford	8,000
Birmingham	30,000	Bolton	5,000
Manchester	30,000	Northampton	5,000
Sheffield	25,000	Newbury	4,000
Hull	22,000	Bradford	4,000
Nottingham	17,000	Chippenham	2,500
Leeds	17,000	High Wycombe	2,500
Chester	15,000		

The figures are very approximate, being based upon rough calculations made at the time by men such as Arthur Young. There was no official census until the next century. Town populations were small, and many towns which are great today were sleepy villages then. Bristol was easily the second largest town after London.

Even the largest towns lacked proper water supplies, paved streets, a police force, and other amenities. Diseases were rampant, and no one knew how to check infection. The ones who suffered most, of course, were the poor; in 1721 a contemporary wrote with disgust of the situation in Manchester, and described how the parish disposed of diseased corpses: "They dig in the churchyards or other annexed burial places, large holes or pits in which they put many of the bodies of those whose friends are not able to pay for better graves; and then, those pits or holes (called the Poor's Holes), once opened, are not covered till filled with such dead bodies. . . . How noisesome the stench is that arises from these holes so stowed with dead bodies, especially in sultry seasons and after rain, one may appeal to all who approach them." Not until industrial pressure increased, at the end of the century, did people really begin to demand sanitary and public health improvements. The following table speaks for itself:

1736 The first public hospital in Winchester.
1749 Liverpool Infirmary opened.

1751 Manchester's first public baths built.

1752 Manchester Infirmary opened.

1765 Newcastle upon Tyne opened its Lying-in Charity.

1771 Norwich opened its first hospital.

1784 Dr. Thomas Percival made his famous Report leading to the creation of the Manchester Board of Health.

1791 First Lunatic Asylum founded at York.

1796 Manchester opened its Fever Hospital.

The blame for slow improvement rests with the primitive state of local government at that time. Manchester and Birmingham were not even properly incorporated as towns then, and the older towns that did boast a Municipal Corporation and Royal Charter lacked any central authority. No one was in charge. The London Parliament lay many miles away and was of little interest to them, except for their jealously guarded right to return Members. Many of the philanthropists and leading merchants were Dissenters, and as such were often barred from taking part in municipal government. The Dissenters most active in this civilizing work included the older groups, such as the Unitarians and Independents, although the Quakers, for example, were active in York.

Not all the leading citizens in the provinces, however, wanted connections with London. There was a growing feeling that provincial life and industry would benefit from a certain freedom. Lord Kinnoul wrote in a letter in 1767, "We see by daily experience the fatal effects of politics upon industry and manufactures; and the great towns of Birmingham, Sheffield and Manchester feel the superior advantage of not sending Members to Parliament, and likewise that of not being hampered with the fetters of the exclusive privileges which corporations enjoy. By these means, genius has free scope, and industry is exerted to the utmost without control, check or interruption."

In this free atmosphere, intellectual life began to flourish. Liverpool was the first provincial town to form a subscription library (1757), and Leeds followed in 1768, with Manchester in 1792. Active "Literary and Philosophical" Societies sprang up in many towns, led by such men as Robert Owen, Joseph Priestley, Richard Price and John Dalton, and became places of reforming zeal. Many members of the old local squirearchy were beginning to apprentice their sons to the new, rich merchant and trading houses, and so the two societies moved closer together. This led to a marked rise in standards of taste – in architecture, music and fine arts, literature, and manners. The provincial stage (as distinct from travelling players or the showmen with their booths) dates from the second half of the century: the Nottingham Theatre (1760) and Manchester Theatre Royal (1775), for example. Newspaper shops and bookshops also flourished by the 1750s, often under the same ownership. Two well-known provincial booksellers were Dr. Johnson's father in Lichfield, and William Hutton, the historian of Birmingham.

The Country Squire

The country squire was by and large an uncouth boor, barely educated,

The country squire was supposed to be happiest when out hunting, or discussing the day's sport with his huntsman, amid trophies of his success

Circulating libraries helped spread to the provinces ideas current in London, increasing the contact between capital and country

and rarely moving far from his land. He spent his time working hard, drinking, swearing and sometimes serving his turn as a local magistrate. One writer noted, "he spends that part of the day, in which he is not on horseback, at table, in smoaking and getting drunk . . . he is naturally a very dull animal." The French observer, the Abbé Le Blanc, believed "the country people in England, to say nothing more, are very clownish and unpolished . . . These honest gentlemen are never easy but in each other's company; and commonly had rather smoak at the steward's table than dine at the master's."

The following description is given by George Crabbe about his great-uncle, Mr. Tovell, a squire who had been to school, and who farmed an estate worth £800 a year: "On entering the house, there was nothing at first sight to remind one of the farm: a spacious hall, paved with black and white marble, at one extremity a very handsome drawing-room, and the other a fine old staircase of black oak, polished until it was as slippery as ice, and having a chime clock and barrel-organ on its landing-place. But this drawing-room, a corresponding dining [room], and a handsome sleeping apartment upstairs, were all tabooed ground, and made use of on great and solemn occasions only . . . At all other times

"New River Water!" The water seller was familiar in city thoroughfares

21

Above "Me and my Wife and Daughter," the town dweller's view of country folk
Below "London Sportsmen shooting:" the townsman's lack of skill at country sports made many laugh

the family and their visitors lived entirely in the old-fashioned kitchen along with the servants. My great-uncle occupied an armchair, or in an attack of the gout, a couch on one side of the large open chimney. Mrs. Tovell sat at a small table, on which, in the evening, stood one small candle in an iron candlestick, plying her needle by the feeble glimmer, surrounded by her maids, all busy at the same employments; but in the winter a noble block of wood, sometimes the whole circumference of a pollard, threw its comfortable warmth and cheerful blaze over the whole apartment."

The Tovells at supper: "If the sacred apartments had not been opened, the family dined on this wise: the heads seated in the kitchen at an old table; the farm men standing in the adjoining scullery, door open – the female servants at a side table, called a *bouter*: with the principals, at the table, perchance some [wandering] rat catcher, a tinker, a farrier, or an occasional gardener in his short sleeves . . ." (George Crabbe). The diet was coarse and unvaried. One contemporary remembers a typical meal of a country squire in these words: "He eats nothing but salt beef, cold mutton, cabbage, carrots and pudding, which last is his [fondest] dish; and that which is heaviest he likes best. His drink is ale, coarse Portuguese wine, and now and then a little of the strongest brandy."

Some landowners were beginning to take great pride in their agricultural methods, and studied very closely the new ideas of improvers like Jethro Tull, Bakewell, Coke of Holkham and others. Men who knew how to put their land to better use soon came to the attention of the great aristocratic landowners anxious to talk to them. One such was a Mr. Wenar. An entry in the *Wynne Diaries* reads: "Captain Fremantle drove me in his gig to see Mr. Wenar's farm, and his famous fat oxen for which he every year gets two or three prizes – he was not at home, but his daughter as fat as the cattle (though a civil girl) [made me a tour] of the mansion which is a very ancient half-ruined house – she showed me the fat beasts which are fed some on oil cake and some on turnips, and look like elephants. It is only in the country that one may see a man like Mr. Wenar, who is visited and courted by Dukes and Peers, dines at their table, and returns their dinners, and all this because he can fatten oxen better than his brethren, the other farmers. A German baron could hardly believe this." The patterns of land use were changing.

The Village Community

We are given a detailed account of life in Borrowdale about 1780, in the book *Pleasure and Pain* (1780–1818). Borrowdale was "a Valley, divided into small & well-cultivated Farms, occupied by the owners; who are the 'Statesmen' of Borrowdale, & live secluded from the World in small neat Houses. . . . Insulated from the Rest of Mankind by Impracticable Mountains, equally unknowing and unknown, they have their own Chapel, their own School & their own Butchers, their cattle for corn, which the Vale will not produce; & in bartering their Wood for Pins, Needles, & the other Productions of the Fine Arts that Peddling Gipsies have to bestow . . . Oh Rousseau! what a retreat was here for the Man of Nature!"

"Cucumbers?" Towns offered a growing market for the produce of the near-by countryside

For a countryman there was greater variety of meat, fish and game, fresher and cheaper than in the towns

Above A country boy sets off to try his luck selling garden produce

Above Blacksmiths were important members of country communities. *Below* Living conditions for poor country people were primitive: chairs and good fires were often unknown

With few and bad roads, the villages of eighteenth-century England were self-contained and inbred. A village had to be able to clothe and feed itself, provide work for all, and look after its old and sick. Conditions had hardly changed since Shakespeare's day. Village women made the clothes – spinning, weaving and sewing. They also baked the bread from locally grown corn, brewed the beer, salted meat for winter and sometimes helped in the fields. The men made nearly all their own equipment, for example axes, shears, knives, saws, spades, hoes, wagons and carts, hurdles for the sheep-pens, woven baskets. They dug stone and chalk for building cottages and barns. Wages, where paid at all, were very low, perhaps 6s. or 7s. a week; most village workers received payment in kind, shelter, corn, milk, sometimes fish, rarely meat, wool. They were at least more or less immune from the wild fluctuations in the price of bread and other products which hit eighteenth-century townspeople so hard. Every village had one or two craftsmen for special jobs, such as a blacksmith, potter, joiner, weaver, maltster or tanner, depending on local needs and resources. Buying and selling with other villages or towns in the same county was rare. Work was hard – up at dawn and to bed at sundown. Children had to help as soon as they were strong enough to hold a broom or carry timber.

Relaxations and pleasures were few, perhaps fishing, snaring rabbits, a little poaching. A visit to the market or fair in a distant town would be an experience of a lifetime.

Those villagers who farmed three or four acres of their own in the common fields could afford a little more independence of the local squire. Those squires who wanted to make improvements to the property by enclosures often complained about it. One wrote, "If you offer them work, they will tell you that they must go to look up their sheep, cut furzes, get their cow out of the pound or, perhaps, say that they must take their horse to be shod that he may carry them to the horse race or a cricket match." In his book *Horse-Houghing Husbandry* (1731), the great agriculturalist Jethro Tull agreed: "The deflection of [workmen] is such that few gentlemen can keep their lands in their own hands but let them for a little to tenants who can bear to be insulted, assaulted, kicked, cuffed and Bridewelled with more patience than gentlemen are provided with ... It were more easy to teach the beasts of the field than to drive the ploughman out of the way."

Rural housing, if such it can be called, was very primitive. Villagers lived in hovels made of stones piled up and covered with thatch or brushwood, or of cheap local materials, such as "mud and stud" in clay districts, or wood on the edge of the great forests such as Wychwood, Wyre, Sherwood, Rockingham, Knaresborough and elsewhere (many of which have since disappeared). The structures were barely weatherproof, and few have survived from Johnson's time into the present century. Brick cottages were unknown until the next century. Cottages were tiny, perhaps one living-room and one bedroom for the entire family. Ceilings were low; the windows were small and without glass, the floor beaten earth, perhaps covered with straw.

Yet to many contemporaries, the English village sometimes seemed set in a Garden of Eden. In *The Deserted Village*, Goldsmith wrote:

Town dwellers held a very romantic view of English villages. They never noticed leaking roofs, smoky hovels, or patched, worn clothes. A scene from an early edition of Goldsmith's *The Deserted Village*

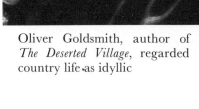

Oliver Goldsmith, author of *The Deserted Village*, regarded country life as idyllic

> How often have I loitered o'er thy green,
> Where humble happiness endeared each scene!
> How often have I paused on every charm,
> The sheltered cot, the cultivated farm,
> The never-failing brook, the busy mill,
> The decent church that topped the neigbr'ng hill,
> The hawthorn bush, with seats beneath the shade,
> For talking age and whispering lovers made.

But this was a particularly rosy view. What does seem clear, however, is that the English village compared extremely well with villages on the Continent in the same period. The young Comte de la Rochefoucauld wrote on his visit to Norfolk in 1784, "As always, I admired the way in which in all these little villages the houses are clean and have an appearance of cosiness in which ours in France are lacking. There is some indefinable quality about the arrangement of these houses which makes them appear better than they actually are."

The Family at Home

Breakfast for most people consisted of just tea and rolls, or bread and

The pump from which everyone had to draw their water

The home of the small country squire was built to withstand time; many still
grace the English countryside

Frying sprats: most cooking
was done on an open fire

butter; sometimes toast would be eaten in winter. Foreigners were
surprised at this dish. C. P. Moritz wrote in 1782: "The slices of bread
and butter given to you with tea are as thin as poppy leaves, but there is a
way of roasting slices of buttered bread before the fire which is incomparable. One slice after another is taken and held to the fire with a
fork until the butter is melted, then the following one will be always laid
upon it so that the butter soaks through the whole pile of slices. This is
called *toast*."

People did not usually breakfast until the day had already begun;
many rose at six but did not breakfast until ten. Fashionable people often
took their breakfast so late that they were able to make calls beforehand;
and in Bath and other spas and resorts the whole business of bathing and
"taking the waters" usually took place before breakfast. In the first part
of the century, breakfast parties were popular. We know from the
Gentleman's Magazine that public breakfast parties were held at such
places as Ranelagh, or Ruchholt near Stratford, or Marylebone Gardens,
or Cox's at Dulwich. Bubb Dodington (1691–1772) the diarist, recorded
a private breakfast party in his *Diary*: "The Princess of Wales and Lady
Augusta attended by Lady Middlesex and Mr. Breton did Mrs. Doding-

A pause for refreshment: mealtimes were variable and for the rich breakfast
was seldom eaten before ten o'clock

ton and me the honour of breakfasting with us. After breakfast, we walked
all round my gardens: we came in, and they went into all the rooms . . .
it was near three o'clock."

Dodington was not the only person to breakfast so late in the day.
Fashionable people thought of the morning as lasting until dinner-time,
say two or three in the afternoon. C. P. Moritz wrote in 1782 that "it was
usual to walk out in a sort of *negligée* or morning dress, your hair not
dressed, but merely rolled up in rollers, and in a frock and boots."

Dinner was the chief meal of the day, eaten at two or three o'clock in
the afternoon, although the rich often did not sit down until four or five.
The Swiss visitor César de Saussure, who was in England between 1725
and 1730, wrote "an Englishman's table is remarkably clean, the linen is
very white, the plate shines brightly, and knives and forks are changed
surprisingly often, that is to say, every time a plate is removed. When
everybody has done eating, the table is cleared, the cloth even being
removed, and a bottle of wine with a glass for each guest is placed on the
table." At this point, the ladies retired, leaving the men to propose
toasts – a long and solemn ceremony – and smoke clay pipes of tobacco.

C. P. Moritz complained bitterly about the poor standard of English

An eighteenth-century London
inn sign

27

An Edinburgh fishwife selling oysters

dinners: "An English dinner . . . generally consists of a piece of half-boiled or half-roasted meat; and a few cabbage leaves boiled in plain water; on which they pour a sauce made of flour and butter." English coffee, he called "a prodigious quantity of brown water." The wheat bread, the butter, and Cheshire cheese, however earned praise. The middle classes were heavy beef- and mutton-eaters, although some people ate fish; and oysters became a delicacy. Parson Woodforde leaves an account of a dinner which included a leg of mutton with caper sauce, a pig's face, a neck of pork roasted with gooseberries, and plum pudding. Delicacies included "potatoes in shells," cold tongue, partridge, roast swan ("good eating with sweet sauce"), Parmesan cheese, orange and apple puddings, syllabubs and jellies.

Supper was the last meal of the day, and included the same sort of dishes that were eaten at dinner. In 1726, César de Saussure noticed that "supper is not considered a necessary meal," but by the end of the century, this had changed, and people liked "a late and great dinner" (Johnson). Ordinary people had their supper at eight or nine o'clock, at

The ugly sisters, "Greed" and "Gluttony," a cartoon published in 1773

A kitchen in a country house

the end of a long day's work, but the rich often ate supper in the small hours, after a dance or party. Horace Walpole commented in 1777, "The present folly is late hours . . . Lord Derby's cook lately gave him warning: the man owned he liked his place [job] but said he should be killed by dressing suppers at three in the morning."

The diet of the poor was very plain. At the start of the century, coarse rye and barley bread was eaten a good deal, although the purer bread made from wheat became more widely available later on. Former luxuries such as tea and sugar now came within the means of many people, causing Arthur Young to refer disapprovingly to the "growth of luxury among the poor." Young took a note of some average prices of food during his tour of 1771: bread $1\frac{1}{4}d.$ a pound, butter $6d.$ a pound,

28

butcher's meat 3*d.* a pound, cheese 3*d.* a pound. These items had to be purchased from wages which were probably only 6*s.* to 8*s.* a week.

Daily life in the eighteenth century was an almost non-stop round of work, and more work. Ordinary people rose at 5 a.m. or 6 a.m. and usually worked through until 8 p.m. or 9 p.m. Those families who were self-employed, and paid piece-work, naturally tended to work long hours to scrape money together; those who were employed by others had to work these hours, or be sacked for "idleness." There was no escape from this routine for children. They were set to work by their parents as soon as they could do anything useful. In towns, very young children might be made to run errands, wash floors, help carry and give other domestic help. In the countryside, they scared birds from the crop fields, picked stones from the soil in readiness for tilling, combed wool and collected rushes for dipping in tallow. Daily life was extremely hard, and children had to play as much a part as the old, sick and destitute in the struggle for existence. There was no idea that children occupied any special place in the home or in society; there were no schools for them to go to, no idea of "education." They were regarded more or less as small adults, and everyone hoped they would grow up as quickly as possible to do their share of work, to learn a useful trade, or perhaps go to sea, as many did, at the age of twelve or less.

Many people felt that the treatment of children was a disgrace to society, and encouraged them to become lawless or idle. One man who decided something should be done was Jonas Hanway, who with the help of Sir John Fielding, and others, founded the Marine Society, which trained poor boys for the sea. He also spoke out against the cruelties of chimney-sweep boys, before the time of Bennet and Shaftesbury. But his main self-appointed task was to rescue pauper children. Having studied poor-houses and foundling hospitals abroad, he became a Governor of the Foundling Hospital in London, and helped bring about the Acts of 1761 and 1767. The Act of 1761 obliged parishes to keep registers of their infant poor. The 1767 Act ("the Hanway Act") made parishes send their pauper children under the age of six into the country to be looked after, at not less than 2*s.* 6*d.* a week. But many parishes had little interest in really helping, and Hanway himself sadly commented, "the apprenticeship of some parish children is as great a scene of inhumanity as the suffering of others to die in infancy."

Marriage in those days was a binding contract for life, always performed by a priest, often at the instructions of the parents. Divorce was extremely rare and difficult to obtain, since it required an Act of Parliament in each case. Bigamy, desertion and other marital offences were probably more common then than now, partly because women had very few rights they could legally enforce against bad husbands, and partly because of the lack of law enforcement. Yet there are more complaints from the husbands than the wives. Johnson thought, "Our marriage service is too refined. It is calculated only for the best kind of marriages; whereas, we should have a form for matches of convenience, of which there are many." He agreed with Boswell, "that there was no absolute necessity for having the marriage ceremony performed by a regular clergyman, for this was not commanded in scripture."

The house-maid in clothes of George III's time

"Gin Lane" by Hogarth, a graphic indictment of the evils of gin-drinking

Boswell wrote a little "epigrammatick song" which Garrick had had set to music, bewailing the fate of husbands:

A Matrimonial Thought

In the blithe days of honeymoon,
  With Kate's allurements smitten,
I lov'd her late, I lov'd her soon,
  And call'd her dearest kitten.

But now my kitten's grown a cat,
  And cross like other wives,
O! by my soul, my honest Mat,
  I fear she has nine lives!

James Boswell, the Scottish lawyer, friend, and biographer of Samuel Johnson

Later, Boswell "mentioned to him a dispute between a friend of mine and his lady, concerning conjugal infidelity, which my friend had maintained was by no means so bad in the husband as in the wife. Johnson: 'Your friend was in the right, Sir. Between a man and his Maker it is a different question: but between a man and his wife, a husband's infidelity is nothing. They are connected by children, by fortune, by serious considerations of community. Wise married women don't trouble themselves about infidelity in their husbands.'"

Gin Drinkers

The first half of the century saw more gin drunk by the people of Britain than at any other time. Gin was not expensive – certainly more within the means of the ordinary person then than now. The order of the day was, "Drunk for 1*d*., dead drunk for 2*d*., straw for nothing;" the amount consumed was enormous. Henry Fielding wrote in 1751 after two years as a London magistrate, "Gin . . . is the principal sustenance (if it may so be called) of more than a hundred thousand people in this metropolis. Many of these Wretches there are, who swallow Pints of this Poison within the Twenty Four Hours: the Dreadfull Effects of which I have the Misfortune every Day to see, and to smell too," he added. The root of the trouble lay in the last part of the seventeenth century; home manufacturers had been encouraged by the Government in making English spirits from corn, to discourage imports. Alehouses had to be licensed by the magistrates, but the sale of gin went unchecked. In London alone there were perhaps 8,000 places where gin was openly sold, apart from alehouses: stalls and barrows, chandlers and tobacconists were some.

Above Cheap brandy made a change from gin

Both drinkers and manufacturers opposed reform; in fact, a £20 retail licence fixed in 1720, and a 2*s*. per gallon duty were lifted in 1733, when wheat-growers protested to Parliament that sales had slumped. But three years later, Parliament returned to the attack, fixing a new licence fee of £50, and a tax of 20*s*. per gallon. In those days, it amounted to virtual prohibition; but due to evasion of payments, violence against informers, and difficulties of administration, Parliament in 1743 again reduced all these charges, though from now on the distillers could not sell their own liquor direct to the public, but had to wholesale it to licensed retailers paying a 20*s*. licence. But outside London, the towns were still very anxious about the effects of gin in increasing lawlessness and idleness, and after Bristol, Salisbury, Rochester, Manchester and Norwich petitioned Parliament a new Act was passed (1751) which stopped the worst excesses. After 1751, the situation began to improve although gin still continued to be as popular a drink as tea is today.

Down and Out

Parishes, of which England had 15,000, were responsible for looking after their own poor (as well as for their sick, aged and orphans). The Government did not concern itself. Most parishes only contained a few hundred people, and so had small resources. Most relied upon the services of an overseer, appointed by the local magistrates. The poor could apply to the parish for "relief," and the overseer then had to decide whether to give them a few pence from the rates and send them on their way; try to find them work; or threaten them with trouble if they didn't find work themselves. Most people of the time agreed with Daniel Defoe, who said that a "pauper given employment was a vagabond given a favour." So it was, that the ratepayers used the parish workhouses as a way of driving idle beggars to find work for themselves.

Under the Poor Law Act of 1722, parishes were allowed to build their own workhouses, and to put their poor to work. Many parishes turned their poor over to a road-builder or other contractor in exchange for a hire fee; a parish would sometimes let a road-builder put a whole workhouse under marching orders. The parish purse would be protected,

Shoeblacks were among the poorest street hawkers

31

the contractor would get workmen – and the poor would probably suffer. As the Quaker John Scott wrote in 1773, "By means of this statute, the parochial managers are impowered to establish a set of petty tyrants as their substitutes, who, farming the poor at a certain price, accumulate dishonest wealth, by abridging them of reasonable food, and imposing on them unreasonable [toil]." The workhouse was often feared as a "House of Terror." As well as the workhouse, there was the poor-house, virtually a doss-house. Crabbe paints a pathetic poor-house scene in *The Village* (1783):

> Theirs is yon House that holds the Parish-Poor,
> Whose walls of mud scarce bear the broken door;
> There, where the putrid vap'rs, flagging, play,
> There Children dwell who know no parents' care;
> Parents who know no children's love, dwell there!
> Heart-broken matrons on their joyless bed,
> Forsaken Wives, and Mothers never wed;
> Dejected widows with unheeded tears,
> And crippled age with more than childhood fears;
> The Lame, the Blind, and, far the happiest they! –
> The moping Idiot and the Madman gay.

Henry Fielding in 1753, in his report on the Poor Law, said, "they starve and freeze and rot among themselves." But Dr. Johnson's complacent views were more typical of people of the time. Boswell described their talk on the subject: "He [Dr. Johnson] said, 'the poor in England were better provided for, than at any other country of the same extent . . . Where a great proportion of the people', said he, 'are suffered to languish in helpless misery, that must be ill-policed [governed] . . . a decent provision for the poor is the true test of civilization.'" In 1750, about £700,000 of parish rates went to the relief of the poor. The middle classes who paid it felt it was a heavy and annoying burden.

Fielding wrote three years later, "Every man who hath any property must feel the weight of that tax which is levied for the use of the poor; and every man of any understanding must see how absurdly it is applied. So very useless, indeed, is this heavy tax, and so wretched its disposition, that it is a question whether the poor or the rich are more dissatisfied . . . since the plunder of the one serves so little to the real advantage of the other; for while a million yearly is raised among the former, many of the latter are starved; many more languish in want and misery; of the rest, many are found begging or pilfering in the streets today, and tomorrow are locked up in gaols and bridewells."

A further attempt at reform was made in 1782, with the passing of Gilbert's Act (Thomas Gilbert, M.P., 1720–98). From now on, the workhouse was to be reserved for the helpless, such as the old, the sick, orphans and unmarried mothers; the able-bodied poor were now exposed to the harsh Vagrancy Laws, under which vagabonds, "unlicensed pedlars" and others faced merciless prison sentences. Towards the end of the century, between 3,000 and 4,000 vagrants a year were sent to houses of correction; but needless to say, as many more were driven to crime. By 1800 there were over 4,000 workhouses and poor-houses in the country.

Above A man loaded with "mischief" (matrimony), a famous London inn sign

33

Opposite top Many great private residences of this period have since become public property, such as this, once Queen Anne's House and now the National Maritime Museum. *Opposite below* Hogarth's painting of polite society. *Left* Dissolute living, from Hogarth's "Rake's Progress." *Below* A musical evening, painted by Hogarth

Right Prisoners brought out for a cold bath in Field's Prison, London. *Below* Inmates of the Fleet Prison, London, were put to useless work on the treadmill

NEWGATE

Top right The duel, a fierce clash of swords and pride. *Top left* The forbidding aspect of Newgate Prison in London. *Left* An inmate of Newgate Prison visited by his family and friends (Hogarth)

"The Election Dinner" by Hogarth, a familiar scene of bribery and debauchery at election time

Above Shipping and trading at Broad Quay on the River Frome. *Right* Overlooking the river at Bristol, the second city of England, from the fort near the town

3 An Industrious Nation

Banking

IN THE eighteenth century, the Bank of England (founded in 1694) offered attractive prospects to the successful merchant or adventurer; after the South Sea Bubble (1720) it had a monopoly of joint-stock (company) banking until the nineteenth century; and there was a ban on any group of more than six persons issuing notes of their own. In the eighteenth century, the Bank came to play an important part in financing new industries and enterprises. First, it provided a safe deposit, which was far more secure than that offered by goldsmiths and silversmiths; it reduced the level of interest by making more capital available; it issued a paper currency of £10, £15 and £20 notes, with the £5 note added in 1794; it kept the gold coinage of the realm in better condition; and it eased foreign exchange.

Farthings minted in Queen Anne's reign

During this century, accounts came to be settled far more by paper bills than they had been previously; moving bullion across country from one merchant house to another was becoming rare. Paper bills were of many kinds – promissory notes, cheques, drafts or bank notes. A bank note, like any other bill, was "a promise to pay," and modern pound notes still bear the words of the Bank: "I promise to pay the Bearer on Demand the sum of One Pound." Paper has since become so accepted that in practice this demand will not be met. By 1700 London had become paramount in handling paper bills; but during the next decades, manufacturers and merchants in the provinces moved more and more into this type of transaction, becoming banker merchants, then merchant bankers. They included the Edinburgh corn-dealer, Coutts; the Norwich worsted manufacturer, Gurney; the Birmingham ironmaster, Lloyd. By 1800 there were almost 400 banks receiving deposits and paying interest, issuing bills for the use of their depositors, and themselves, and making money by discounting bills for cash. These banks did much to make commercial life flow more smoothly, lending money for agrarian enclosures or factory expansion, and putting local capital fully to use. Paper money was not at this time normal domestic currency. The lowest denomination was £10, which might be a workman's wages for half a year. Small transactions were carried out in groats, farthings, halfpennies and pennies, with copper coin, or silver and gold for larger amounts.

The Bank of England, London (1743)

The trade label of the South Sea Company

Caricature of the South Sea Bubble (1721)

The South Sea Bubble

The South Sea Company was formed in 1711 to trade with South and Central America, then controlled by Spain, in the hope that the Spaniards would permit it. The Treaty of Utrecht did grant some trading rights, but these were so small it is hard to understand the mad rush which apparently made the country wish to buy shares in the Company. It was as if everyone belonged to a conspiracy to keep buying, to force the price of the shares higher and higher. Some, indeed, did make their fortunes. The Duchess of Ormonde told Jonathan Swift: "Now the King has adopted it [the South Sea Bubble] and calls it 'his beloved child;' though perhaps you may say, if he loves it no better than his son it may not be saying much. But he loves it as much as he does the Duchess of Kendall and that is saying a good deal!" Prior wrote that "I am lost in the South Sea: the roaring of the waves and the madness of the people are justly put together. It is all wilder than St. Antony's dream." As another contemporary put it, "Statesmen forgot their Politics, Lawyers the Bar, Merchants their Traffic, Physicians their Patients, Tradesmen their Shops, Debtors of Quality their Creditors, Divines the Pulpit, and even the Women themselves their Pride and Vanity." Those who sold their stock early on reaped large financial gains; but those who held on imagined themselves to be wealthy too. Smollett wrote: "Luxury, vice and profligacy increased to a shocking degree. The adventurers, intoxicated by their imaginary wealth, pampered themselves with the rarest dainties and the most costly wines . . . All party distinctions, religion, sex, character and position, were swallowed in this yawning abyss . . . Gambling was the sole profession."

This sudden interest in stocks and shares was quite new. The *London Journal* of the time noted: "The hurry of stockjobbing has been so great this week as to exceed all ever known. Nothing but running about from coffee-house to coffee-house, and subscribing without knowing what the proposals were. The constant cry was, 'For God's sake let us subscribe to something; we don't care what it is.'"

"We are informed," writes one journalist, "that since the hurly-burly of stockjobbing, there has appeared in London 200 new Coaches & Chariots, besides as many more now on the Stocks in the Coach-makers' yards; above 4,000 embroider'd Coats; about 3,000 gold watches at the sides of whores and wives; and some few private acts of charity." A few weeks later "'tis credibly reported that a little Fellow, call'd Duke, a Change Alley porter, has got about £2,000 by the Bubbles and is about to set up his chaise with a handsome Equipage."

The collapse, when it came, was violently sudden. "Ruin and bankruptcy were universal." Lord Molesworth in the House of Lords, like many other people, blamed the company directors, saying they should be tied in a sack and thrown into the sea. Many leading people were prosecuted – Craggs, the Secretary of State and Aislabie, Chancellor of the Exchequer were convicted of taking bribes. Hundreds of people were ruined, and many found themselves thrown into debtors' prisons.

The bursting of the South Sea Bubble gave a bad name for decades to "gambling" in shares and stock; Dr. Johnson defined a jobber as "a low wretch." The cautious preferred landownership; others lent money for road improvement to the turnpike trusts, who offered the toll income as security; others invested in the canal boom after 1760. The old companies, such as the Bank of England, East India Company, Hudson's Bay Company and Africa Company all offered secure investments, and the overall market for investments grew better as the century passed. In 1773 the dealers who had traded in Change Alley at Jonathan's Coffee-House moved to Threadneedle Street, and hung a sign over the door with the inscription, "The Stock Exchange." Rules were made, a sixpenny admission charge was levied, and share-dealing slowly became respectable.

Above Jonathan's Coffee-House, London's unofficial Stock Exchange

The Merchant

The supremacy of English commerce at this time is shown in this extract from *The British Directory* (1791): "The commerce of the world being in perpetual fluctuation, we can never be too watchful . . . Who could have imagined three hundred years ago that those ports of the Levant from whence [we] were supplied with the spices, drugs, etc. of India and China, should one day come themselves to be supplied with those very articles, by the remote countries of England and Holland, at an easier rate than they were used to have them directly from the East . . . At present, our woollen manufacture is the finest in the Universe, and second to it is our metallic manufacture of iron, steel, copper, tin, lead and brass, which is supposed to employ upwards of half a million of people."

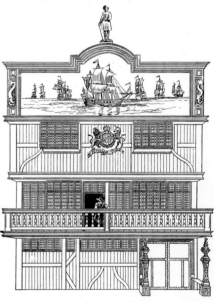

Above The Old South Sea House in London

Below Warren Hastings, first Governor-General of India, originally went there on East India Company affairs

The largest single trading company was the giant East India Company, with trading posts, offices and private armies in many corners of the globe. The two East India Companies of the late seventeenth century were merged in 1708, receiving a monopoly of the East India trade by various Acts of Parliament. In return, the new Company made large loans to the Government at low interest. It had about twenty ships, up to 499 tons (it avoided tonnage of 500 and over, as such ships had to employ a chaplain). It imported raw silk, cotton yarn, undyed calicoes, as well as tea from China, and coffee from Surat or Mokha. *The British Directory* (1791), noted: "Our trade to the East Indies [is] one of the most stupendous political and commercial machines that is to be met with in history . . . through the various internal revolutions which have happened at Indostan, and the ambition and avarice of their servants and officers, acquired such territorial possessions as render them the most formidable commercial republic [since] the demolition of Carthage. Their revenues are only known, and that but imperfectly, to the Directors of the Company, who are chosen by the proprietors of the stock." But later in the century, repeated troubles beset the Company and its management of India which was bitterly attacked by Fox and Burke.

Textile Workers

Wool was traditionally "the staple manufacture of the country," protected by Parliament. High duties discouraged the import of wool,

Spinning wool, a cottage woman's task. On the left wool is spun to thread, on the right it is reeled with the clock-reel, and over the fire it is boiled

Below Samuel Crompton, inventor of the spinning mule (1776). *Bottom* Irish linen industry in 1783: tilling, sowing, harrowing for the summer's flax crop

and penalties the export of wool for weaving on foreign looms. Despite the growing popularity of cotton fabrics, and damage to exports caused by wars, wool exports prospered, rising from £3 million in 1720 to £5 million in 1790. The men and women of the West Country clothed the upper classes, Yorkshire the masses (challenging the old supremacy of East Anglia for worsted). The Yorkshire and Lancashire weavers were the first to take up the new machines such as the spinning-jenny and Kay's "flying shuttle;" Lancashire was the main home of textiles, based on the "triangular trade" – cottons out to West Africa, slaves from West Africa to the West Indies, cotton, sugar and tobacco from the West Indies back to Liverpool.

With the coming of machine-spinning, Whitney's gin and the machines of Crompton, Hargreaves and Arkwright, cotton exports rose from £14,000 in 1739 to over £300,000 in 1779. New sources of power were being used – water and steam as well as hand and animal power. At the end of the century, many industries were still based in homes, not factories. In his book *The State of the Poor* (1797) Eden noted, "in the north, almost every article of dress worn by farmers, mechanics and labourers is manufactured at home, shoes and hats excepted."

The independent worker, who owned his own tools and materials, bought and sold his own stock, and worked at home, became rare as the years passed. He would buy the wool at the weekly market, which his wife and children made into yarn; then he and his sons wove it into cloth, perhaps helped by apprentices or journeymen; and after fulling it at the mill, took it to the town market or cloth-hall to sell. A man could set up in a small way without too much expense. A Joseph Broadbent of Huddersfield in 1779 had two spinning-wheels at 5s. each, "looms and gears" at 24s., a pair of worsted looms at 10s. 6d., and a spinning-jenny at £2 10s. and other equipment together worth only £9 12s. 6d. In *The London Tradesman* (1747) R. Campbell said that eight master trades only needed £5 capital, ten needed £10, twenty-five needed £20, ninety needed £50 and seventy-five needed £100.

A man who prospered could soon find himself as a "merchant" with a London agent or office to buy and sell his wool, dozens or hundreds of people on his pay-roll, working at their homes or in his factory, and with banks or other merchants willing to lend him money to expand. A really successful clothier might employ 500 to 2,000 or 3,000 people.

A successful trader might decide to build a factory, and bring his workers out of their homes under his direct control. A Huddersfield clothier in 1806 was typically down to earth: "principally to prevent embezzlement of cloth and tool, but if we meet men we can depend upon for honesty we prefer having [the cloth] woven at their own houses." Some employers thought factories would make life better for the workers; Lombe's silk-mill in 1783, for example, employed "about two hundred persons of both sexes and of all ages to the great relief and advantage of the poor," who might otherwise be out of a job. Factories also saved time and money on transport. But many ordinary folk detested the idea of factory bells, having people over them, and working from 6 a.m. to 8 p.m., so it was, that even until 1800, industrial life showed great variety.

Scenes of the woollen industry first printed in the *Universal Magazine*
(1749). *Top left* sheep are sheared of their fleece, *bottom right* the wool is
combed out, worked *top right* and finally beaten *bottom left* before being spun

From Rags to Riches

"Men are every day starting up from obscurity to wealth," said Dr.
Johnson. Most of the great eighteenth-century factory-owners and
merchants had poor origins. Men prepared to work and experiment
with new methods faced few barriers to success – no income or profits tax,
a population which in England and Wales rose from 5,500,000 in 1700
to 9,178,980 by the 1801 census, an export trade which doubled between
1714 (over £7 million) and 1760 (over £14 million), and the growth of
banking and credit facilities. All classes of people welcomed the new
climate: "There was never from the earliest ages a time in which trade so
much engaged the attention of mankind, or commercial gain was sought
with such general emulation. The merchant is now invited to every port,
manufactures are established in all cities, and princes who just can view
the sea from some single corner of their dominions are enlarging [docks],
erecting mercantile companies, and preparing to traffick in the remotest
countries." (Dr. Johnson in his Preface to Rolt's *New Dictionary of Trade
and Commerce*, 1756.)

The Militant Tailors

All clothes were handmade; there was no mass production by machines,
though many garments were sold ready-made. Fashionable tailors took
care to dress like gentlemen of the day, in order to show off their handi-
work and encourage high fashion; Colley Cibber, in *Love's Last Shift*
(1696) wrote, "One had as good be out of the World as out of the Fashion."

Tailors' Hall, Threadneedle
Street, London, headquarters
of the militant tailors' guild

James Potter,
Leather - Breeches Maker.

At the Sign of the Boot *and* Breeches, *within Three Doors of* Aldgate, *on the Left Hand Side of the Way, in* Shoemaker-Row.

Maketh and Selleth all Sorts of Leather-Breeches, by Wholefale and Retail, at Reafonable Rates. Likewife Buck and Doe Skins and all Sorts of Leather for Breeches.

Printed at the Old Katherine-Wheel without Bifhopfgate.

A tailor and breechmaker's advertisement

The craft of the tailor has not changed much in essentials over the generations; in the eighteenth century as at other times, his work mainly involved cutting, sewing, and fitting and measuring his client (as in the Hogarth print of 1735, showing the young master come to take his inheritance). Sometimes, for comfort's sake, a tailor would wear working clothes consisting of a banyan (a kind of elegant *negligée*) and a nightcap.

The tailors were the first craftsmen really to try and set up a trade union. In London in 1744, no less than 15,000 journeymen tailors and stay-makers formed a "combination" or union to raise their wages beyond the levels laid down by Act of Parliament. An earlier combination of 1720 had had some success, with 7,000 men uniting, and new wage levels being set. But if the levels were exceeded, master tailors could – and were – fined £5 each time, and might have their licence, and so their livelihood, taken away. The tailors' loud claims of "rights" under Magna Charta did them no good. Combinations were illegal, although the law did guarantee a minimum wage, and protect journeymen against the employment of non-freemen. But things remained unsatisfactory. Frequent petitions to Parliament from master tailors show that while they were willing enough to keep to the wage levels, their men were restive, and often violent, to the damage of the trade. Payments in Middlesex for instance of 2s. a day in winter and 2s. 6d. in summer, though high by the standards of the day, did not satisfy the journeymen tailors.

There was a brisk trade in cast-off clothing, sold mainly by pedlars who walked the streets of towns and villages, or visited fairs and markets. Many working people never had new clothes, yet looked clean and smart. C. P. Moritz thought in 1782 that the English were a well-dressed people: "Not a man pushing a wheelbarrow but he has his white underclothing, and hardly a beggar can be espied who doesn't wear a clean shirt under his tatters."

Drapers

Here is a visit to a London draper's shop in 1715: "This afternoon, some ladies, having an opinion of my fancy in clothes, desired me to accompany them to Ludgate-hill, which I take to be as agreeable an amusement as a lady can pass away three or four hours in. The shops are perfect gilded [places], the variety of wrought silk so many changes of fine scenes, and the mercers are the performers in the opera; and

"Buying new clothes:" drapers sold fewer ready-made garments than lengths of material

instead of the *vivitur ingenio* you have in gold capitals, 'No trust by retail.' They are the sweetest, fairest, nicest, dished-out creatures; and by their elegant and soft speeches you would guess them to be Italians. As people glance within their doors, they salute them with, 'Garden silks, ladies! Italian silks, very fine Mantua silks, any right Geneva velvet, English velvet, velvet embossed?' And to the meaner sort: 'Fine thread satins, both striped and plain; fine mohair silks, satinnets, burdens, Persianets, Norwich crapes, silks for hoods and scarves, hair camlets, druggets, sagathies, gentlemen's nightgowns ready-made, shalloons, durances, and right Scottish plaids!'"

The Cloth Fair in London, named after the annual tailors' and drapers' fair held there

"We went into a shop which had three partners: two of them were to flourish out their silks and the other's sole business was to be gentleman usher of the shop, to stand completely dressed at the door, bow to all the coaches that pass by, and hand ladies out and in. We saw abundance of gay fancies, fit for sea-captains' wives, sheriffs' feasts, and Taunton-dean ladies. 'This, madam, is wonderful charming. This, madam – ye Gods! would I had 10,000 yards of it!' Then gathers up a sleeve, and places it to our shoulders. 'It suits your ladyship's face wonderfully well.' When we had pleased ourselves, and bid him ten shillings a-yard for what he asked fifteen: 'Fan me, ye winds, your ladyship rallies me! Should I part with it at such a price, the weavers would rise upon the very shop. Was you at the Park last night, madam? Your ladyship shall abate me sixpence. Have you read the *Tatler* to-day?'"

"These fellows are positively the greatest fops in the kingdom," the lady added, "they have their toilets and fine nightgowns; their chocolate in the morning, and their green tea two hours after; turkey-polts for their dinner; and their perfumes, washes and clean linen equip them for the Parade."

These were some of the materials for sale in a draper's or man's mercers in the year 1774: "Dutch ratteens, duffles, frizes, beaver coatings, kerseymeres, forrest cloths, German serges, Wilton stuffs, sagathies, namkeens, Silasia cambricks, Manchester velvets, silks, grograms, double allapeens, silk camblets, barragons, Brussels camblets, princes stuffs, worsted damasks, silk knitpieces, corded silks, and gattias, shagg velvets, serge desoys, shalloons, and allapeens."

Apprentices and Craftsmen

Apprenticeship was still regulated by the Statute of Apprentices (1563) from the time of Queen Elizabeth I, but in the eighteenth century it was a dying institution. In many of the urban crafts, apprenticeship was still the rule, the apprentice going to stay in his master's house, his master being responsible not only for his training in work, but in good manners too. Several people important in English social and commercial life had served apprenticeships, for example Robert Owen, who was first apprenticed to a Stamford draper. A good master was able to do much to give his apprentices an education, in an age when there were very few schools. On the other hand a bad master could turn out poor apprentices who were liable to join the violent town mobs that became so prevalent later in the century.

The fashionable man was the tailor's delight (1794)

Apprentice weavers (Hogarth): hours were long and the work tedious, so overseers were needed to stop idling

Above London apprentice boy. *Below* Fire was a menace in coking, which this device was meant to reduce

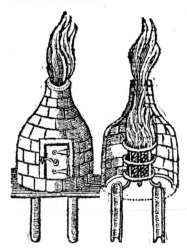

Apprenticeship was strongest in the older crafts, especially those involving long periods of training such as printing. The Statute of Apprentices did not apply to some of the newer industries, for example the cotton industry, although apprenticeship could be entered into. Apprenticeship could cost a poor family a great deal of money: the apprentice would not earn very much, and if he were to stand a chance of success he would later need to buy tools, fit out his own workshop, and employ apprentices or journeymen of his own. An apprentice's conditions of work would depend very much on his master; but wherever he worked, the hours would be very long by modern standards, often 6 a.m. to 8 p.m. Also, during the seven years of their indenture, most apprentices had to do almost anything their masters might tell them. In fact, Josiah Tucker declared in 1757 that he thought the relationship between man and master was "much nearer to that of a Planter and Slave in our American Colonies than might be expected in such a country as England."

Coal, Iron and Steel Workers

About 200,000 men worked in the iron industry in 1719; but the industry looked in a bad way, due to the shortage of charcoal for the blast-furnaces. In 1720, only about fifty-nine blast-furnaces existed, producing about 18,000 tons of pig-iron a year; but in 1788 the figure had risen to 68,000 tons, and by 1806, 250,000 tons. Improvements included coking, puddling (Henry Cort), and labour-saving machinery such as Newcomen's steam-engine, used by Abraham Darby in 1743, and John Roebuck's improved bellows (1761). The blast-furnacemen converted the crude iron into carburized liquid iron, running it into ladles and pouring it into casts, where it cooled as cast-iron pots, grates, tools and so forth. In some works, the liquid iron was run into D-shaped furrows, or "pigs," the cooled iron being known as "pig-iron;" it was converted into square blocks which other workers hammered and

Coal-mining in 1788 at the mouth of a pit near Broseley

rolled. This "bar-iron" then went to the blacksmith who turned it into wrought iron at his forge. Steel-making had always been a problem, as the iron burned with the charcoal had never given a brittle enough metal; but from the 1740s, John Huntsman's steel crucible brought a new era in steel production; he himself moved to Sheffield, helping it to become the leading city in steel production.

Coal-mining was an ancient industry. Coal had long been used for brewing and distilling, brick-, tile- and pottery-making, and the manufacture of nails, hardware, glass, brass and lead and iron-smelting. Defoe wrote that coal was rarely seen in London, owing to the cost of transport, although by 1727 about 700,000 tons a year were needed for London; the coal came by sea from Newcastle and Sunderland, rising in price from 13s. 6d. to about £3 on the way. In 1727, about 30,000 men were employed in the coal industry as miners, seamen and lightermen.

A coal wagon at the pithead being pulled along rails

Although Newcomen's pumping-engine had revolutionized coal-mining in the first part of the century, it was not until the Canal Age began – the Duke of Bridgewater's canal from Worsley coal-field to Manchester was built in 1759 – that the real industrial impetus was given to the industry. Ashton writes that: "More than half the growth in the shipments of coal and the mining of copper, more than three-quarters of the increase of broadcloth, four-fifths of that of printed cloth, nine-tenths of the export of cotton goods, were made in the last eighteen years of the century." As the coal industry expanded, more and more families were drawn from village to mine. "The coal-mining industry had a barbaric life peculiar to itself. Scottish miners were still, in effect, serfs bound to the pits in 1799: in Somerset they were like an alien community planted in the countryside." (J. Steven Watson, *The Reign of George III*.) Only in Durham and Northumberland did the miners work at any depth (maximum 1,000 feet); the Yorkshire pits were only about 300 feet deep. Groups of men worked with primitive picks and crowbars, often not mining as we know it today, but scraping off the coal from outcrops in the countryside. Wood supports for mine roofs were only introduced

"Small Coal!" was a well-known street cry

49

about 1800. The Davy Safety Lamp was not introduced until 1815. Men, boys, women and girls often had to carry coal-baskets on their backs and climb along to get the coal out of the mine; ventilation was poor, and dangerous if coal-gas was present. As the industry grew rapidly after 1790, conditions became more and more cramped and dangerous, and it began to occur to people that it was a social disgrace.

Factories and mines involved accidents and disease, as Howlett wrote in the *Gentleman's Magazine* (1782): "The collier, the clothier, the painter, the gilder, the miner, the makers of glass, the workers in iron, tin, lead, copper, while they minister to our necessities or please our tastes and fancies – are impairing their health and shortening their days." Workers were "suffocated in mines and pits, or gradually poisoned by the noxious effluvia of metals, oils, powders, spirits, &c., used in their work." Howlett adds that they "exhibit as mournful a scene of blinded and lame, of enfeebl'd, decrepit, asthmatic, consumptive wretches, panting for breath and crawling half alive upon the surface of the earth." Until the great industrial legislations in the next century the worker had virtually no security, protection or compensation for injury.

Chimney-Sweeps

Everyone knows the terrible evils of chimney-sweeping in the eighteenth and nineteenth centuries. It is ironic that the boys most often put into that dirty and unhealthy trade were the smallest and youngest, in other words the ones most likely to suffer; it was long recognized as an undesirable practice by decent people, and a Committee on the Employment of Boys in Chimneys (1817) described the abuses in detail. These are some extracts:

"That They are *stolen* from their parents, and *inveigled* out of workhouses; . . . That in order to overcome the natural repugnance of the infants to ascend the narrow and dangerous chimneys, to clean which their [toil is] required, *blows* are used; . . . That *pins* are forced into their feet by the boy that follows them up the chimney; in order to compel them to ascend it; and that *lighted straw* has been applied for that purpose; . . . That the children are subject to *sores* and *bruises*, and *wounds* and *burns* on their thighs, knees and elbows.

"They are kept almost entirely destitute of education, and moral or religious instruction; they form a sort of class by themselves, and from their work being done early in the day, they are turned into the streets to pass their time in idleness and depravity; thus they become an easy prey to those whose occupation it is to delude the ignorant and entrap the unwary."

Yet nothing was done for them in the eighteenth century. People took more pride in their elegant chimneys than in their social conscience.

Above City "Tronmen," Scottish chimney-sweeps. *Top* Glassmakers enjoyed little protection from their furnaces. *Far right* Chimney-sweeps also acted as dustmen. *Below* Chimney-sweeps going to work

Travel

Roads were now relatively safe and increasingly filled with traffic. Most people who moved about were engaged on business – merchants or their agents, judges, lawyers, clerks, Government officials, sheriffs and others. But the eighteenth century saw many more people taking to the roads for the pure pleasure of discovering the countryside.

Celia Fiennes, a celebrated English traveller, wrote in 1702: "If all persons, both Ladies, much more Gentlemen, would spend some of their tyme in Journeys to visit their native land, and be curious to inform themselves and make observations of the pleasant prospects, good buildings, different produces and manufactures of each place, with the variety of sports and recreations they are adapt to, would be a *souveraign remedye* to cure or preserve from these epidemick diseases of vapours," and, "should I add, Laziness?"

She strongly urged menfolk to take a greater interest in their island. "But much more requisite is it for Gentlemen in general service of their country at home or abroad, in town or country, especially those that serve in Parliament, to know and inform themselves the nature of Land, the Genius of the Inhabitants, so as to promote and improve Manufacture and Trade . . ."

The threat to security posed by the Jacobite Rebellion of 1745, however, emphasized the need to build good roads, especially to open up communications in Scotland. Around the mid-eighteenth century, many Turnpike Acts were passed, improving the system founded by the Turnpike Acts of 1663 (Hertford, Cambridge and Huntingdon) and 1695 (for the London–Colchester route). Turnpike Trustees were appointed to raise money at the toll-gates and devote it to repairs and maintenance of the roads; they also checked the weight of vehicles at toll-gates, and numbers of horses and wheels used; weighing-machines at toll-gates were compulsory within thirty miles of London. Innkeepers were not allowed to act as Turnpike Trustees.

Travel was often awkward and uncomfortable, but sedan-chairs offered a gracious alternative for town journeys

Throughout the century, the toll-gates caused mob violence: people resented having to pay, resented the bureaucracy, resented the time lost on a journey, and resented the special privileges of the gentry (the gentry never had to pay the extra tolls imposed in 1741 on vehicles over three tons: exemptions included gentlemen's carriages, farmers' vehicles, and wagons in the King's service). An Act of 1728 laid down a penalty of three months' imprisonment and whipping for a first toll-gate offence, and seven years' transportation for the second: the death penalty was added later. Yet the *Gentleman's Magazine* of 1749 reported that in Bristol "about 400 Somersetshire people cut down a 3rd time the turnpike gates on the Ashton road . . . then afterwards destroyed the Dundry turnpike, and thence went to Bedminster, headed by two chiefs on horseback . . . the rest were on foot, armed with rusty swords, pitchforks, axes, guns, pistols, clubs."

Complaints about the lack of improvement of turnpike roads continued throughout the century. An official Middlesex Report of 1798 recorded: "Most of the *parish highways* in this county are superior to any other of equal extent I have ever seen . . . gentlemen may ride along them, even

Various styles of carriage, the covered coach

The open-sided, back-to-back cart

An open, inward-facing pony cart

directly after rain, and scarcely receive a splash. The *turnpike roads* on the contrary are generally very bad; although at the tollgates of this county there is collected . . . not less than £130,000 a year, which is uselessly expended in sinking wells, erecting pumps, building carts and hiring horses and men to keep the dust down, by watering, instead of more wisely scraping it off." If the situation was bad in London, it was even worse in remote areas: in the first half of the century there was not a single turnpike in Devon, Dorset or Cornwall, until the Exeter Turnpike Trust was set up in 1753, responsible for roads 150 miles in each direction. The improvements which could now be afforded cut the London–Exeter coach time from four days to two.

Coach Travel

This was a journey by stage-coach in the mid-eighteenth century: "This ride from Leicester to Northampton I shall remember as long as I live . . . My companions on top of the coach were a farmer, a young man very decently dressed, and a blackamoor. The getting up alone was at the risk of one's life, and when I was up, I was obliged to sit just at the corner of the coach, with nothing to hold by, but a sort of little handle fastened on the side . . . the moment that we set off, I fancied that I saw certain death await me . . . The machine now rolled along with prodigious rapidity, over the stones through the town, and every moment we seemed to fly into the air; so that it was almost a miracle that we still stuck to the coach and did not fall. At last . . . I crept from the top of the coach and got snug into the basket. 'O sir, you will be shaken to death!' said the black; but I flattered myself he exaggerated . . . when we came to go down hill, then all the trunks and parcels began as it were, to dance around me . . . I was obliged to suffer this torture nearly an hour till we came to another hill again, when quite shaken to pieces and sadly bruised, I again crept to the top of the coach and took possession of my former seat." (Moritz, 1782.)

The post-chaise was a faster, more comfortable, but more expensive means of travel. Its advantages were discussed in *The Sussex Advertiser* (1791): "There are two modes of conveyance, either by common stages or by a post-chaise. By the common stage you are classed with company of every description, and who may very frequently turn out to be disagreeable. You are also paid no attention to at the inn where you stop, although you pay exorbitant for refreshment, and are frequently insulted by the indecent [language] of the coachman, and besides your fare you have a considerable sum to pay for luggage. On the contrary, if two or three passengers choose to travel together, they may, by [proceeding] in a post-chaise, not only avoid all these inconveniences – but suit their own convenience in point of time, and be at less expense – besides meeting with gentler treatment at the inns on the road."

This is how a stage-coach looked, according to a contemporary observer: ". . . covered with dull black leather, studded by way of ornament with broadheaded nails, with oval windows in the quarters, the frames painted red . . . The roof rose in a high curve with an iron rail around it. The coachman and guard sat in front upon a high narrow boot . . . Behind was an immense basket supported by iron bars . . . The machine groaned and creaked as it went along."

Drunken driving seems to have been a hazard then as now. One case was reported in a Bristol newspaper of 1770: "The London Mail did not arrive so soon by several hours as usual on Monday, owing to the mailman getting a little intoxicated on his way between Newbury and Marlborough, and falling from his horse into a hedge, where he was found asleep, by means of his dog."

An average day's journey in the middle of the century was fifty or sixty miles, and over a hundred by the end of it. But really fast times captured the public's imagination. This table gives examples of fast times in the 1750s:

Newcastle to London (1785) Three days (cut from six days in 1754)
Birmingham to London (1785) Nineteen hours (two days in 1752)
Manchester to London (1788) Twenty-eight hours (cut from four and a half days in 1754)

Fares varied a good deal, and it is difficult to generalize. Rates depended on whether the journey was made by post (express) or ordinary wagon; but the amount of custom was the main factor. Thomas Somerville wrote in 1779: "I returned to Scotland . . . in the beginning of June . . . it shows the increased expense of [journeys], that we paid no more than 7d. per mile for posting from London to York. Finding the horses not so good, we paid 9d. per mile (which was the ordinary charge) for the remaining part of the journey. The duty on posting (2d. per mile) did not commence till July 1, 1779." And when he repeated the journey in 1800, the cost had almost doubled yet again. A common summer rate was $2\frac{1}{2}d.$ per mile in 1769, and 3d. in winter, on account of the greater difficulties of the roads.

Carriage and chairs jostle for space outside St. James's Palace in London

"Difficulties of departure:" preparing to leave a country inn for London Town

Below Exaggerated wheels of private carriages in George III's reign

Above A hackney coachman rests his horses beside a London square

Above A popular inn sign of the time, and *below* the yard of the Tabard Inn

Exploring England was a considerable adventure, especially for foreign tourists. C. P. Moritz was one of many who complained of hostile treatment at the hands of native Englishmen in the countryside. César de Saussure agreed with him. In 1727 he wrote, "I do not think there is a people more prejudiced [towards themselves] than the British people, and they allow this to appear in their talk and manners. They look on foreigners in general with contempt, and think nothing is as well done elsewhere as in their own country."

Inns and Innkeepers

Inns greatly improved as road travel grew in the eighteenth century, and reached a peak of excellence in the reign of George III. Building and rebuilding went on constantly. "People at this period, 1770, were rebelling against antique discomfort. The rooms of the average inn at this time were [covered] in deal, but the furniture in the best rooms was of mahogany. Hence it was that the curtains – rep and chintz – together with extra candles and the needlework bell-pulls, came to be charged on the bills. It was at this time that [bypassers] insisted on the use of the warming-pan before venturing between sheets." (A. Groom, *Old London Coaching Inns and Their Successors*.) Inns were of traditional design – courtyard with arched entry, reception hall, main staircase, coffee-room and dining hall; sometimes they included small private apartments known by names such as Sun, Moon, Star, Crescent or Paragon. The great city inns which served as coach terminals were splendid places – for instance the George and Blue Boar in Holborn, London (coaches direct to Glasgow), which had forty bedrooms, stabling for fifty-two horses, seven coach-houses and a drive seventy yards long.

Food varied a good deal; at the Lion in Liverpool, "a very good supper consisting of veal cutlets, pigeons, asparagus, lamb and salad, apple pie and tarts" could be had for only 6*d*. (*Journey Through England*, 1752 by "An Irish Gentleman"). But catering was a problem in the coaching inns with coaches arriving and departing at all hours of the day and night, hungry and thirsty passengers demanding to be fed.

We have an excellent picture of the times from the notes of contemporary accounts, such as Moritz's *Journeys of a German in England*, and Defoe's *Tour Through the Whole Island of Great Britain*. Moritz grumbled about a room at Windsor which "much resembled a prison for malefactors," and a few miles further on at Slough, referred to "this impudent ill-usage of people, who ought to reflect, that they are but servants of the public." Tipping was usual, although Moritz stormed out of more than one inn complaining of the bad service. Landlords themselves were often pillars of the community, stage-coach owners and postmasters. At election times their local support could be extremely valuable to the politically ambitious, and many innkeepers became prosperous men, no doubt feeling themselves superior to the complaints made by passing visitors, of which the commonest was "dirty". A good inn was a beacon in the wilderness. Said Dr. Johnson, "There is nothing which has yet been contrived by man by which so much happiness is produced as by a good tavern or inn."

Highwaymen

A highway robbery which took place on 26 June 1750 was set down by a contemporary: "An exact representation of Maclaine the Highwayman robbing Lord Eglington on Hounslow Heath on the 26th June 1750... Maclaine is said to be born in the north of Ireland, of Scotch parents, is a tall genteel young fellow and commonly very gay in his dress. On the 27th July last, he was apprehended for a robbery on the Highway and committed to the Gatehouse, Westminster, by Justice Lediard; among others whom he robbed was Lord Eglington. The stratagem he made use of was very extraordinary, being as follows: On the 26th June, as his Lordship was going over Hounslow Heath early, Maclaine and his companion, knowing they should have a good booty, resolv'd to rob him. But as he was well armed with a blunderbuss some contrivance was necessary. They therefore agreed that one should go before the post-chaise and the other behind it; he before the chaise stopped the Postilion, and screened himself in such a manner that his Lordship could not discharge his blunderbuss at him without killing his own servant; at the same time Maclaine, who was behind, swore if his Lordship did not throw the blunderbuss out of the chaise, he would blow his brains through his face. His Lordship, finding himself thus beset, was forced to comply and was robbed of his portmanteau and 50 guineas. His Lordship had two servants half a mile behind."

In fact, there seem to have been fewer highwaymen in the eighteenth century than legend would have us believe. Many people were certainly robbed on highways, but the villains nearly always lacked the romance which is attributed to them by novelists. The culprits for distorting the facts include the innkeepers of the time, who knew that to advertize their inn as the haunt of a famous highway-robber would increase custom from curious coach passengers passing that way. Even if there were no obliging highwaymen in evidence, the landlord would often invent

The notorious highwayman Maclaine robs Lord Eglington on Hounslow Heath just outside London

Above "Mulled Sack," one of the much-feared robbers who plagued highways. *Below* Dick Turpin, probably the most famous of all highwaymen

and embroider incidents to his customers' fearful satisfaction. It is true, though, that the crowded throng in coaching-inn yards often concealed thieves on the look-out for passengers with valuables or money, of which they could be robbed when their coach had run a few miles out of town. Some legends have a basis of truth. "Gentleman Harry," for example, is known to have been an Old Etonian, who made his headquarters first at the White Swan in Whitechapel, and later at the Saracen's Head in Aldgate. Others included Dick Turpin, alias John Palmer, Hawke, and another known as "Mulled Sack." Another, Jack Rann, was a dandy who wore sixteen tassels at his knees, to show he had been in prison sixteen times.

London footmen, especially in the early eighteenth century, had a bad reputation as highwaymen, or for acting in partnership with them to rob their masters. It was not necessary to go far out of London to find deserted spots to commit a crime; many people lost their purses and baggage on the great heaths and commons – Hounslow, Putney, Richmond, Barnes, Hampstead and elsewhere. But it was a dangerous occupation, since many people armed themselves with pistols or blunderbusses for security, and went accompanied with servants.

The Grand Tour

At least once in his life, the eighteenth-century English gentleman went on the Grand Tour, usually to France and Italy, but almost never to Germany or the American Colonies. Although England and France were at war much of the time, the international friendships of the ruling classes hardly suffered; Englishmen were as warmly greeted in French *salons* and Italian Courts, as at home. The Tour usually lasted about a year, and was the experience of a lifetime, developing new friendships, and exchanges of views and influences in art, literature, music and philosophy.

Adam Smith, however, did not think much of the Grand Tour. In *The Wealth of Nations* (1776) he wrote: "In England, it becomes every day more and more the custom to send young people to travel in foreign countries immediately upon their leaving school, and without sending them to any university . . . In the course of his travels a young man generally acquires some knowledge of one or two foreign languages; a knowledge, however, which is seldom sufficient to enable him either to speak or write with propriety. In other respects he commonly returns home more conceited, more unprincipled, more dissipated, and more incapable of any serious application, either to study or to business, than he could well have become in so short a time had he lived at home."

As many of the English upper classes were educated in Italy, the Italian influence came to be felt in architecture and design. Lord Burlington, as leader of the "Grand Tourists," became patron of the new building which was closely fashioned after the villas of Palladio in Vincenza, and patron of artists in the Italian school; if this style died after his death it was to be replaced by more Italian influences, this time of ancient Roman archaeology (Herculaneum had been discovered in 1719, and Pompeii in 1748).

Above The English Channel is crossed by air for the first time (1785)

Country folk eating dinner at an inn – the fare is simple, bread, boiled ham and beer. Notice the hatch into which the barrels of beer were unloaded, the thatched roof and leaded window-panes

59

Canaletto's famous view of the River Thames, with Greenwich Hospital in the background

Brooks's Club in St. James's, the
exclusive gambling room

Top Skating on the River Thames in winter. *Right* A showman with peepshow and squirrel at a London fair. *Far right* Punch and Judy, always a popular attraction at fairs

4 Amusements and Diversions

Fairs

SEVERAL IMPORTANT FAIRS took place each year during the eighteenth century, not only in and around London, but in other towns such as Bristol, Bath, Oxford, Winchester and elsewhere. Fairs brought together thousands of people of all classes from the surrounding countryside – merchants, tradesmen, entertainers, quacks and mountebanks, sightseers, pickpockets and thieves. Originally, fairs were serious commercial events, but by the time of the eighteenth century they had become excuses for a holiday, and sometimes in this lawless age for "riot and debauch." To study a fair of this period is to study its people.

Held in August each year, St. Bartholomew's Fair was mainly a cloth fair. The merchants exhibited their cloth inside the Priory which was closed at night and reopened in the morning. Over the years, however, the Fair developed into a general market where whole streets of booths exhibited objects of every kind, lace, gold and silver ware, jewelry and fineries, and, as the Fair attracted a wider custom, toys, walking-sticks, buttons, hosiery, second-hand clothes, gingerbread, food and drink. Sports also took place, including wrestling contests and shooting-matches, which satisfied the strong eighteenth-century penchant for gambling mixed with danger, all this against a background of "Shrill fiddling, sharp fighting, and shouting and shrieking. Fifes, trumpets, drums, bagpipes, and barrowgirls squeaking."

As always with public meetings in those days, law and order presented a problem, and in 1769 the Mayor appointed seventy-two special constables, as well as banning plays and gambling. But violence, robbery, and even murder, were committed much as before. The Fair became an increasing nuisance towards the end of the century, and in 1798 it was proposed to ban it; but this was not done until a generation later.

St. Bartholomew's Fair, like others, featured many entertainment booths with curious exhibitions at 3d. or 6d., such as of wild beasts, freaks and dwarfs, strange inventions, quack doctors and puppet-shows. The showmen would cry out, "Rar-ee-show!" Some of the great theatrical booths, run by such names as Penkethman, Mills, Booth and Doggett, put on spectacular plays and dramas with finely costumed actors. The novelist Henry Fielding started his career as part-owner of one such

Wrestling and boxing always afforded entertainments at fairs

For the dishonest showman fairs promised good business

Southwark Fair in London, full of wonders, freaks and disasters for the poor to gape at

Powell's famous puppet-shows at Covent Garden were more popular than services at the local church

booth, where he stayed for nine years in company with the popular comedian, Hippisley.

Another celebrated showman was Faux, a conjurer and posture-master who died worth £10,000. One of his tricks is described in the *Gentleman's Magazine* of February 1731. His booth was visited by Algerian diplomats, and at their request he showed them a view of Algiers, "and raised up an apple tree which bore ripe apples in less than a minute's time, which several of the company tasted of." Another booth contained a number of freaks and monsters, always fascinating to the public: "A prodigious monster with one head and two distinct bodies," or "An admirable work of nature, a woman having three breasts," or again "A child alive, about a year and a half old, that has three legs." Other oddities included pigs which could do arithmetic, play cards and tell fortunes; admission at these "wild beast" shows, which were always so popular, became expensive, rising as high as 1s.

For generations, "frost fairs" were held on the River Thames whenever it froze over; this frequently happened, sometimes enough to allow a coach and six to drive over (as in 1698), but always enough to attract citizens, showmen, piemen, barbers and anyone else who had something to sell. The last traditional frost fair was held in the winter of 1813–14; after Old London Bridge had been pulled down, the freer-running river made freezing a thing of the past.

Actors and Playgoers

Plays were the one amusement of the day which never grew stale or went out of fashion. London playhouses opened in the eighteenth century included the Haymarket (1705) by Vanbrugh, and Covent Garden promoted (1733) by John Rich. In theory, the stage was regulated by the Lord Chamberlain who could give and take back licences as he chose, shut playhouses for six weeks on the death of the King, and sometimes throw actors in prison; the Master of the Revels, another official, could censor scripts, and take a fee of 40s. for every new play produced (until the playwright Colley Cibber challenged it). But in the eighteenth century there was almost no one to enforce the law, and so plays and playhouses sprang up without licence. At last, the Government brought in a Licensing Act (1737), but it was scorned by Lord Chesterfield: "It is our duty to encourage and protect wit, whosoever's property it may be," and pointed out that "the Lord Chamberlain is to have the [fortune] of being chief gauger, supervisor, commissioner, judge and jury." But the Act did not have much effect, despite its aim to have only two stages in London – Drury Lane and Covent Garden.

Newspapers were actually anxious to pay for the privilege of advertizing plays – sometimes as much as £200 – as it helped their circulation. The great eighteenth-century actor, David Garrick, was said to be the first to print his own name in larger letters on an advertisement, showing that he "topped the bill." Performances generally began at 6 p.m., with prices much as in Pepy's time a century before – boxes 4s., pit 2s. 6d., first gallery 1s. 6d. and upper gallery 1s. Stalls were not introduced until 1829. In the first part of the century, footmen were allowed into the upper gallery free, to stop them hanging about noisily in the corridors outside, waiting for their masters and mistresses to come out; but they annoyed everyone who had paid for their admission so much, that in 1737 the Manager of Drury Lane announced the end of the privilege (in verse):

> They've grown a nuisance beyond all disasters.
> We've none so great but their unpaying masters.
> We beg you, Sirs, to beg your men that they
> Would please to give us leave to hear the play!

After a riot in which thirty footmen and stage employees were arrested, the Manager had his way. Otherwise, the pit was the next noisiest place. Wrote Pope:

> The Many-Headed Monster of the Pit
> A senseless, worthless and unhonour'd crowd
> Who, to disturb their betters might proud,
> Clatt'ring their sticks before ten lines are spoke,
> Call for the Farce, the Bear, and the Black Joke.

Yet the pit became "the chosen home of the critics." As in earlier times, the rich sat on the stage, but in pews at the side, well clear of the actors. The auditorium was lit by candles in the boxes and on the pillars of the

Above Drury Lane, one of the two licensed London playhouses

Above A rich actor in his chair

Below Playbill advertizing the famous actor David Garrick at the "top of the bill"

The Laſt Time of the Company's performing this Seaſon.
At the Theatre Royal in Drury-Lane,
This preſent MONDAY, June 10, 1776,
The WONDER.
Don Felix by Mr. GARRICK,
Col. Briton by Mr. SMITH,
Don Lopez by Mr BADDELEY,
Don Pedro by Mr. PARSONS,
Liſſardo by Mr. KING,
Frederick by Mr. PACKER,
Gibby by Mr. MOODY,
Iſabella by Miſs HOPKINS,
Flora by Mrs. WRIGHTEN,
Inis by Mrs. BRADSHAW,
Violante by Mrs. YATES.
End of Act I. The Grand GARLAND DANCE,
By Signor GIORGI, Mrs. SUTTON,
And Mr. SLINGSBY.
To which will be added a Muſical Entertainment, call'd
The WATERMAN.
The PRINCIPAL CHARACTERS by
Mr. BANNISTER,
Mr. DAVIES,
And Mr. DODD.
Mrs. WRIGHTEN.
And Mrs. JEWELL.
To conclude with the Grand Scene of The RECATTA.
Ladies are deſired to ſend their Servants a little after 5 to keep Places, to prevent Confuſion.
The Doors will be opened at HALF after FIVE o'Clock.
To begin at HALF after SIX o'Clock. Vivant Rex & Regina.
The Profits of this Night being appropriated to the Benefit of
The Theatrical Fund, the Uſual Addreſs upon that Occaſion
Will be ſpoken by Mr. GARRICK, before the Play.

Above and below David Garrick, actor and playwright

Below Happenings on the stage were not the only diversions playgoers could enjoy

surrounds; there were no footlights. Darkness in the evenings accounts for the 6 p.m. performance times. But in 1765, Garrick introduced candle footlights in place of the old candelabra over the stage. Costumes were splendid, quite unnecessarily so, being mostly the gifts of noblemen to their chosen actors and actresses.

Officially, everyone held the acting profession in contempt; actors were regarded as vagabonds, and actresses as whores; yet in private society, the most famous players were on intimate terms with the nobility. Standards of acting and stage management greatly improved in this century; and Garrick contributed a more easy and natural style to actors' speech, in place of the old-style declamations.

One of those who knew Garrick well was little Fanny Burney, for the famous actor often visited their house to see her father, the musician. Garrick, it seems, used to call on the Burneys so early in the morning that Fanny was often not up to see him: "Mr. Garrick to my great confusion, has again surprised the house before we were up. But really, my father keeps such late hours at night that I have no resolution to rise before eight in the morning . . . I dressed myself immediately, but found he was going as I entered the study . . . He said with a very comical face to me, 'I like you! I like you all! I like your looks! I like your manner,' and then, opening his arms with an air of heroics, he cried, 'I am tempted to run away with you all, one after another.' We all longed to say, 'Pray do!'"

Garrick, incidentally, was a great mimic of Dr. Johnson. Boswell explained why: "He was always jealous that Johnson spoke lightly of him. I recollect he exhibited him to me one day, as if saying, 'Davy has some *convivial pleasantry* about him, but 'tis a *futile fellow*;' which he uttered perfectly with the tone and air of Johnson."

C. P. Moritz visited the Haymarket playhouse in 1782, and took a note of the prices: "It costs five shillings for a seat in a box, three shillings in the pit, two shillings in the circle and one shilling in the gallery; and the gallery certainly makes the most noise for its shilling. I sat in the pit . . . every moment a rotten orange came whizzing past me or past my [companion]; one hit my hat, but I dared not turn round for fear one hit me in the face . . . there is no end to their shrieking and banging with sticks until the curtain goes up. I have seen a tall baker's boy reaching over the rails and beating with his stick on the outside of the gallery with all his might, visible to everyone but quite unabashed . . . Behind me in the pit sat a young fop who continually put his foot on my bench in order to show off the flashy stone buckles on his shoes; if I didn't make way for his precious buckles, he put his foot on my coat tails." Play-going was one of the few legitimate outlets for high spirits.

Gamblers

Gambling played a large part in club life, especially in the later part of the century. At Almack's Rooms, for example, where a ten-guinea subscription covered twelve meetings, stakes were high; often as much as £10,000 in gold coin lay upon the green tables. Superstitious gamblers wore their coats inside out for good luck. Others protected the insides of

The Government cashed in on the gambling craze by running State lotteries at the Mercers' Hall in London

their expensive lace ruffles with leather patches. While the men gambled, the women preferred to dance; the atmosphere was select and genteel, and the rules of good manners strictly observed. Early in the next century no less a personage than the Duke of Wellington was turned away, for the social crime of wearing trousers instead of knee-breeches. Other clubs which were scenes of gambling included Brooks's, founded by a wine-merchant, and Crockford's, founded by a fishmonger's son. The games of chance included hazard, loo and whist.

Gambling was classless, indulged in by great and small. The Duke of Cumberland was an inveterate gambler, and the women were often as bad. In 1761, Horace Walpole recorded: "In less than two hours t'other night, the Duke of Cumberland lost four hundred and fifty pounds at Loo, Miss Pelham won three hundred, and I the rest." But gambling for much larger sums was common. Walpole wrote in disgust in 1770 that the gaming was "worthy the decline of our Empire, or Commonwealth, which you please. The young men of the age lose five, ten, fifteen thousand pounds in an evening." At White's, the same club, "Lord Stavordale, not yet one-and-twenty, lost eleven thousand there last Tuesday, but recovered it by one great hand at hazard: he swore a great oath – 'Now, if I had been playing *deep*, I might have won millions!'" A foreign visitor, Le Blanc, noted how often gambling expressions had begun to appear in common speech, such as, "Ten to one it isn't true!"

The Government decided to exploit the universal craze for gambling by holding State lotteries. These were usually held in Mercer's Hall, Ironmonger Lane, Cheapside, London. A dignified official in black robes presided; the winning tickets were drawn by blue-coat boys from revolving drums on a large platform. The public crowded in, and fashionable people could hire boxes for the best view of the draw. It is said that, in 1718, excitement in the lottery was so great that £1,500,000 was subscribed. Private lotteries, however, were suppressed by Act of Parliament in 1745.

Gambling (together with gin-drinking) was one of the biggest vices of the time. People gambled and wagered to the limits of their fortune,

and beyond. Gambling added excitement to almost every sport and pastime, including cock-fighting, the duel, prize-fighting and coach-racing. Idle costermongers would gamble at card-games or pitch-and-toss, or play shove-halfpenny. Many philanthropists repeatedly urged an end to gambling, to protect the poor from the workhouses, or from being thrown into Newgate Prison as debtors. The increasing popular influence of Wesleyanism and Nonconformist Evangelism towards the end of the century at last helped to check it.

Newgate Prison where most convicted debtors were sent

Cock-fighting

This account of a cock-fight was given by a Swiss visitor to England (César de Saussure) on 23 February 1728: "The animals used are of a particular breed; they are large but short-legged birds, their feathers are scarce, they have no crests to speak of, and are very ugly to look at . . . The stage on which they fight is round and small. One of the cocks is released, and struts about proudly for a few seconds. He is then caught up, and his enemy appears. When the bets are made, one of the cocks is placed on either end of the stage; they are armed with silver spurs, and immediately rush at each other and fight furiously. It is surprising to see the [zeal], the strength, and courage of these little animals, for they rarely give up till one of them is dead . . . the noise is terrible, and it is impossible to hear yourself speak unless you shout . . . Cocks will some-times fight a whole hour before one or the other is victorious."

Cock-fighting was the most popular sport of the day with rich and poor alike. The rich bred Black-reds, Duckwings and Piles specially for cocking, and even the villager had his "shake-bag." Contests were fought between villages, between counties, between individuals. Steel or silver spurs were introduced at the end of the seventeenth century, to be fastened to the birds' legs. These were expensive. In 1698 the Duke of Rutland paid £3 for six pairs; "long-heel" spurs measured two or two and a half inches long, "short heels" one and a half inches. Other types included sickle, lame, and pen-knife spurs. The simplest was a curved needle; those who could not afford them found other ways of preparing their birds – such as filing their beaks to a very sharp point.

An elimination contest was described as a "main" and would involve any number of birds from seven upwards – always an odd number, to give a winner. Forty-one was a popular number of cocks to put in one main. A long main might last four days, a short one two or three. A "battle royal" was the most ferocious type of contest, in which several cocks were pitted together in one free-for-all. The results of important mains, sometimes held on race-tracks at the height of the racing season, were regularly announced in *The Racing Calendar*; gambling flourished. Under the old "Rules and Orders for Cocking" drawn up in the time of Charles II, birds had been matched by measurement, but during the eighteenth century they came to be matched by weight. Cock-pits varied from elaborate and large arenas with banked seats, to a mere hole in the ground; or two cocks might be shaken out (hence "shake-bag") on to the earthen floor of a village inn. A cock hatched in a magpie's nest was thought to be the stronger, one of many superstitions about the sport.

Facing page Cock-fighting, a very popular sport, often involved gambling for high stakes

71

Visiting spas became a popular craze, though this cartoon of Bath suggests
that fashion had its price

Spas and Resorts

The eighteenth century saw the rise of many new towns. Most – such as
Liverpool, Manchester and Birmingham – owed their fortune to new
trades and industries. But others became popular purely as holiday
places for the rich and leisured. They included Tunbridge Wells,
Harrogate, Knaresborough, Cheltenham, Bath – and a host of new
seaside resorts. But it was Bath above all that attracted the world of
fashion.

The cathedral city of Bath became a popular resort right at the
beginning of the century. Its first Pump Room was opened in 1704, its
first playhouse in 1707, and its first Assembly Rooms (Harrison's) in 1708.
Although Bath was far from London, the influence of Beau Nash and
others gave it quite the most frequent coach service in the country. Bath
was noted for its health-giving waters: enthusiasts would bathe early in
the morning, and join the throng at the Assembly Rooms for a breakfast
of tea and rolls or toast; the sick and hypochondriac then went with
friends and relatives to the Pump Room to drink the waters, and then
perhaps to morning service in the Abbey. The English writer, Celia
Fiennes, enthused about the healthful effect of Bath's waters in getting
rid of "noxious vapours." But she regarded visits to Bath as a duty rather

than a pleasure: "The baths in my opinion makes the town unpleasant, the aire thicke and hot by their steem, and by its own situation so low encompassed with high hills and woods."

She left us an extremely vivid account of the baths themselves: "There are such a number of Guides to each bath, of women to wait on the ladyes and of men to waite on the gentlemen, and they keepe their due distance. There is a Serjeant belonging to the baths that all the bathing tyme walkes in galleryes and takes notice order is observed, and punishes the rude, and most people of fashion sends to him when they begin to bathe, then he takes particular care of them, and complements you every Morning, which deserves its reward at the end of the Season."

Ladies of fashion in George III's reign

As for the waters: "... the water is so strong it will quickly tumble you down; and then you have two of the men guides goes at a distance about the bath to cleare the way. At the sides are rings that you may hold by and so walke a little way, but the springs bubbles up so fast and so strong and are so hot up against the bottomes of ones feete, especially in that they call the Kitching in the Kings bath, which is a great Cross with seates in the middle and many hot springs riseth there."

The hot pumps were specially reserved for the lame and palsied: "I saw one pumpt, they put on a broad brim'd hatt with the Crown cut out, so as the brims cast off the water from the face; they are pumpt in the bath. One of the men guides the pumps, they have two pence I think for 100 pumps, the water is scalding hot out of the pump ... the Ladyes goes into the bath with garments made of a fine yellow canvas, which is stiff and made large with great sleeves like a parson's gown. The water fills it up so that it is borne off that your *shape* is not seen. It does not cling close as other linning [linen] which lookes sadly in the poorer sort that go in their own linning."

A current fashion drawn by the famous artist Gainsborough

Bath offered much besides – riding, walking, reading or hiring newspapers, joining subscription libraries, browsing in bookshops, visiting haberdashers or other shops. In the evening there were balls, stage shows, and parties, thronging with the intimate social life which drew more and more people there. Until 1745 when gambling was made illegal, betting on card-games and sports was very popular; it still continued in private in taverns and lodgings after 1745, but not on the racecourses which were becoming popular in the surrounding district.

Many new seaside resorts were springing up: Margate, Brighthelmstone (later known as Brighton), Weymouth and Scarborough. A popular town since the last century, Scarborough was the most frequented, and was much written about for the health-giving qualities of its water, for instance in Sir John Floyer's *History of Cold Bathing* (1734). Drinking the seawater was widely recommended, and many people – already unwell – suffered agonies in swallowing it, and paid dearly for bottles of salt water sold by quacks. It is amazing to think how primitive the state of medicine was then; yet it has often been said that not until the eighteenth century did the English really become civilized, and feel they were beginning to leave behind the worst barbarities. Brighthelmstone in Defoe's day was only a ramshackle fishing village, but already in 1750 Pococke said it was "greatly improved of late by the concourse of people who come to it to bathe and drink the sea-water." At Margate, Pococke

Bagnigge Wells in 1780, a popular spa on the outskirts of London, once the
summer residence of Nell Gwynn

noticed "the conveniency of covered carriages, at the end of which there
is a covering that lets down with hoops, so that people can go down a
ladder into the water, and not be seen, and those who please may jump in
and swim." The eighteenth century was a curious mixture of flamboyance
and modesty. Deal, Eastbourne and Portsmouth were other seaside
towns or villages that grew into prosperous resorts.

The best-known inland spas were Tunbridge Wells, Harrogate,
Knaresborough, Bagnigge Wells, Cheltenham and Matlock. C. P.
Moritz, who visited Matlock Bath on his 1782 tour, wrote: "The
situation at Matlock itself surpassed all I had expected of it. On the right
were several elegant houses for those taking treatment for their ailments
at the baths . . . on the left ran the river in a deep ravine . . . There is
a great deal of traffic here – on horseback and by carriages – because of
the proximity of the baths." Bagnigge Wells, once the home of Nell
Gwynn, became famous in 1760 when two mineral springs were discovered. The springs were advertised in the *Daily Advertisement* in July
1775: "Mr. Davis, the Proprietor, takes this method to inform the
Publick, that both the Chalybeate and Purging Waters are in the
greatest perfection ever known, and may be drank at 3*d.* each person, or
delivered at the Pump Room at 8*d.* per gallon. They are recommended
by the most Eminent Physicians . . . Ladies and Gentlemen may depend
upon having the best tea, coffee, hot leaves, &c." In an age having little
formal entertainment, the spas were fun.

5 Disease and Medicine

Afflictions

The poorer inhabitants of the eighteenth century lived in deplorable conditions. Streets and towns were unplanned, except to crowd as many houses and tenements as possible into a small area, leaving narrow, unhealthy, unlit and unventilated passages and courts. The window tax, stiffened in 1746, discouraged sunlight and fresh air. Water was unpurified, and gin-sellers often did brisker business than water-carriers; the drains and sewers were open, for example the River Fleet, carrying the filth and garbage of London. Lavatories were placed over open cesspools which often overflowed. Rubbish was just left to rot on the stairs and in the streets (since rubbish collections could only be afforded by the rich).

The importance of personal hygiene was not understood; Sir John Floyer's *Inquiry into the Right Use of the Hot, Cold and Temperate Baths in England* which ran to six editions between 1697 and 1722 does not once mention bathing for the sake of cleanliness. Baths were extremely rare. There was one at Hampton Court, built at the time of William and Mary; St. Bartholomew's Hospital in London was given a swimming-bath in 1736; the City of Edinburgh in 1778 apparently only had three, all at the Royal Infirmary.

In these circumstances, the number of epidemics in the eighteenth century is not to be wondered at. "Jail fever" was common in the crowded, diseased precincts of prisons. In May 1750, the court at the Old Bailey itself went down to jail fever, "killing judges, counsel, and others to the number of forty, without making allowance for those of a lower rank whose death may not have been heard of." The plague, however, had more or less died out by the middle of the eighteenth century. Owing to the lack of medical knowledge of the time, and lack of post-mortems, it is hard to differentiate between the many different kinds of fever. Nor was death registration, or certification of disease, effective over the whole country.

Smallpox, however, was easily identifiable. Curiously, it seems to have been the disease of the upper classes. In 1713, Dr. Emmanuel Timoni mentioned the value of inoculation to Dr. Woodward, Professor of Medicine in London, which he said had been practised successfully in

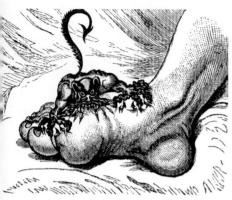

Gout: a contemporary cartoon of the bane of the Englishman's life

Asia for forty years. Nothing was done, however, until 1721, when Lady Mary Wortley Montagu persuaded King George II to order the inoculation of six prisoners in Newgate. Since these and other inoculations worked, inoculation came to be requested more and more by the upper classes. Then, in 1746, the Middlesex County Hospital for Smallpox was founded, and others between 1750 and 1768, although they did not take children under seven years old. But progress was slow, and not until the end of the century did Edward Jenner (1749–1823) first vaccinate from cowpox (1796), and even then, there was considerable opposition to the idea of inoculation.

Gout, an extremely painful complaint, was much discussed and satirized in the eighteenth century, partly because it was popularly put down to too much drink and debauch. Gout is a paroxysmal disease, which inflames the smaller joints, especially that of the big toe. It was customary to swathe the foot in thick layers of bandages. The word gout derives from *gutta* (Latin: "a drop") a reference to the medieval theory of the elements flowing down to the feet.

The following table shows the causes of deaths in the City of London in 1770:

Abortive and stillborn	696	Imposthume	5
Aged	1,512	Inflammation	79
Ague	1	Itch	—
Apoplexy and suddenly	223	Jaundice	156
Asthma and phthisic	590	Leprosy	2
Bedridden	9	Lethargy	6
Bloody Flux	—	Livergrown	2
Bursten and Rupture	12	Lunatic	90
Cancer	42	Measles	115
Canker	1	Miscarriage	6
Chicken pox	1	Mortification	199
Childbed	172	Palsy	69
Cholic, gripes, and twisting of the guts	48	Pleurisy	13
		Quinsy	6
Cold	7	Rash	2
Consumption	4,809	Rheumatism	4
Convulsions	6,156	Rickets	4
Cough and whooping-cough	249	Rising of the Lights	—
Diabetes	1	St Anthony's Fire	—
Dropsy	1,024	Scurvy	3
Evil	15	Smallpox	1,660
Fever, malignant fever, scarlet fever, spotted fever, and purples	2,273	Sores and ulcers	24
		Sore throat	22
		Stoppage in the stomach	14
Fistula	9	Surfeit	—
Flux	8	Swelling	1
French pox	65	Teeth	809
Gout	91	Thrush	69
Gravel, stone, and stranguary	34	Tympany	1
Grief	3	Vomiting and looseness	10
Headache	2	Worms	8
Headmouldshot, horshoehead, and water in the head	22		

Surgical aids were primitive, a crutch for the lame, an ear trumpet for the deaf

Bedlam

Henry VIII had granted the religious house of St. Mary of Bethlehem to the City of London as a hospital for lunatics. The new Bethlehem ("Bedlam" for short) was built in Finsbury Square, London, in 1675, and for two centuries it was open to the public. Bedlam, in fact, with its 150 inmates, was one of the sights of London, and the thousands of visitors each year paying 2d. each admission produced some £400 a year extra revenue for the hospital. But during the eighteenth century, at least until 1770, there was no treatment for the inmates; Bedlam was merely a place for detention. Visitors wandered about unattended in the wards, teasing and annoying the patients, and making a public exhibition out of them. Dr. Johnson visited Bedlam on 8 May 1775, and noted a man furiously beating his straw bed. He identified him as William, Duke of Cumberland, punished for his atrocities in Scotland nearly thirty years before.

William, Duke of Cumberland, ended his life as a "lunatick" in Bedlam

The keepers were ignorant, violent men, who habitually chained, whipped and starved the "prisoners." In 1766, the Governors felt that the sightseers were behaving so badly that "the doors be kept locked on public holidays against all visitors;" but the keepers could be bribed, and so in 1770 the rules were made much stricter, "that the admission of visitors be henceforth only by ticket and that accredited visitors be accompanied by an attendant."

Inmates of lunatic asylums were first referred to as "patients" in 1700, but not until the opening of St. Luke's Hospital under Dr. Battie in 1750 were pupils encouraged to study mental illness. Incurable patients were admitted to St. Luke's from 1754, and new buildings were put up in 1782. A greater emphasis was laid on kindness and patience in dealing with the patients, but not until the time of Freud in the following century did mental illness begin to be understood.

The Medical Profession

In previous centuries, the barber had acted as surgeon, but in 1745 the Company of Barber Surgeons was dissolved, and the Surgeons' Company formed. The 1740s, in fact, mark the beginning of scientific surgery. In October 1743 a young Scots surgeon, William Hunter (1718–83), began a course of lectures in anatomy in Great Windmill Street, London, which for the first time included the pupils' dissection of a body themselves, and learning the practical techniques of surgery. (Previously, anatomy was only studied from books and lectures.) Together with his brother John, he converted surgery "from a trade into a science." John Hunter's work is today exhibited in the Museum of the Royal College of Surgeons in London. John Hunter (1728–93), however, was perhaps the greatest figure in eighteenth-century surgery. His achievement in making surgery an experimental science raised the social status of the surgeons, one of whom said at the time, "He alone made us gentlemen."

Surgery was still very hazardous, though. There were no anaesthetics, and no knowledge of infection. As a result, surgery was only resorted to if the patient was already at death's door, or if he was in such pain any-

John Hunter, the Scots surgeon whose pioneer work helped make surgery respectable

way that he would hardly notice the operation. No one enjoyed surgery, least of all the surgeons. One surgeon, John Abernethy, almost never managed to operate without vomiting. Cheselden, another, wrote, "If I have earned any reputation I have earned it dearly, for none ever endured more anxiety before an operation. Yet from the time I began to operate all uneasiness ceased, and if I have had better success than some others, I do not impute it to more knowledge, but to the happiness of a mind that was never ruffled or disconcerted and a hand that never trembled during an operation." The patient was usually heavily dosed with brandy, but was never tied down, although the surgeons' assistants stood close by to exercise "restraint." The tolerance of pain was probably greater [in those days], when people lived more out of doors, and were more hardened to violence and pain. Speed was essential, though. Many operations could be performed swiftly, causing heavy sweating, but no fainting. William Cheselden, for example, the most expert surgeon of his generation, often extracted a stone from the bladder in under thirty seconds. He was Surgeon to St. Thomas's Hospital in London. But many people died on the operating-table, despite every effort. Alexander Pope, the satirist, thought Cheselden a great man:

> Late as it is I put myself to school,
> And feel some comfort not to be a fool;
> Weak though I am of limb, and short of sight,
> Far from a lynx and not a giant quit ,
> I'll do what Mead and Cheselden advise
> To help those limbs and to preserve those eyes.
> Not to go back is somewhat to advance,
> And men must walk at least before they dance.

The eighteenth-century physician usually graduated at a university, and became a Fellow of the Royal College of Physicians if he practised in London. Graduation from university entailed reading a thesis (in Latin), and often an oral examination which might last four or five hours, with refreshments. The oral examination was held in an international language – Latin – as many foreign students took it before the Royal College of Physicians, and many English physicians took it abroad, especially at the University of Leyden. At Oxford and Cambridge, medical degrees could often be bought or otherwise secured by corruption. The physician was in effect a general practitioner to those who could afford his fees. If an operation had to be carried out, the physician attended, but left the work to a surgeon; if drugs or medicines were needed, these were obtained from an apothecary. In the early eighteenth century physicians were held in great respect, and the more fashionable ones, such as Radcliffe (founder of the Radcliffe Infirmary, Oxford) and Richard Mead (1673–1754), earned large incomes. The work of the physician was to study the patient's symptoms and pronounce the cure.

The Freemen of the Society of Apothecaries in London acted as family doctors to the middle and working classes, for smaller fees than the physicians. There was considerable rivalry and jealousy between the physicians and apothecaries; the apothecaries envied the larger incomes and more fashionable work of the physicians; the physicians wanted to

"The Doctor at Dinner," a cartoon suggesting that doctors deliberately spread disease to gain patients and fees

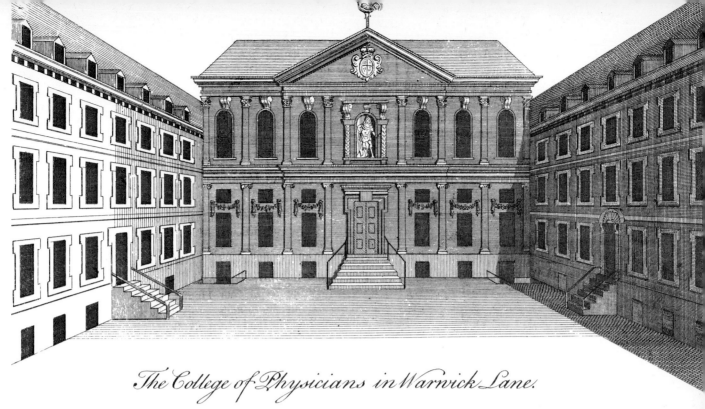

The College of Physicians in Warwick Lane.

The Royal College of Physicians in London. An older branch of medicine
than surgery, there was much rivalry between the two

take over part of the apothecaries' work in dispensing drugs and opening
out-patient surgeries. In 1687 the physicians had fitted up such a surgery
in their College in Warwick Lane, London. The apothecaries objected
violently at this challenge to their profession, and refused to make up
the physicians' prescriptions. There followed the wordy and rather
disgraceful "battle of the Dispensaries," with legal action and propaganda, such as Dryden's rude lines on the apothecaries:

> From files a random recipe they take
> And many deaths from one prescription make.

But in 1724, after much hostility the physicians closed their dispensary,
nevertheless loudly reminding everyone that untrained men (the
apothecaries) could not be relied upon to produce the best medicines.

Members of the College of
Physicians considered themselves socially superior to surgeons

In Hospital

In Dr. Johnson's lifetime, a great wave of philanthropy arose, and from
it emerged the system of county hospitals. London had traditionally been
served by St. Bartholomew's and St. Thomas's, but five other important
hospitals were established during the eighteenth century in London:

    1720 Westminster Hospital.
    1724 Guy's Hospital.
    1733 St. George's.
    1740 The London Hospital.
    1745 Middlesex Hospital.

Altogether well over a hundred new hospitals were built in the period

1700–1800, including the first one in Bristol (1735). They were built and paid for mostly by wealthy private individuals who sought to reduce the sickness and suffering of the time.

At first, all these hospitals were free to any person who was ill, provided he brought a letter of recommendation from a governor or patron. In small towns outside London, this caused no special problem, but in the crowded metropolis, the uneducated poor might not be able to get through the increasing formalities. At St. Bartholomew's, a new patient without a letter had to deposit 19s. 6d. for burial fees (which he got back if he recovered). This would be spent as follows:

Beadle, for giving notice of death to relatives	1s.	0d.
Porter, for parish burial certificate	1s.	0d.
Corpse-bearers, for carrying body to hospital gate "and no further"	2s.	0d.

Opposite top The Foundling Hospital in London, *middle* St. Bartholomew's Hospital in 1752, *bottom* the Royal Hospital, Chelsea, in London. *This page* A scene in a hospital of the time

Matron, for hire of black pall	1s.	0d.
Steward, for death certificate	1s.	0d.
The hospital	13s.	6d.
TOTAL BURIAL FEES	19s.	6d.

But it was also expensive to have an operation at St. Bartholomew's. This table shows the fees due:

Sister of the Cutting Ward [operating-room] for dressings, *etc.*	2s.	6d.
Assistant nurse	1s.	0d.
Ward sister for extra duties	1s.	0d.
Beadle, for carrying patient between ward and cutting room		6d.
Assistant to the Beadle		6d.

The medical profession, pictured by contemporary cartoonists. *Above* dentistry was extremely primitive, though perhaps not as bad as transplanting these teeth suggests, *opposite above* anatomy students at a class conducted before the President of the Royal College of Physicians, *opposite below* doctors were still imagined to use magic ingredients like a unicorn's horn in their pills and potions, *below* the undignified struggle of barbers and surgeons for social recognition

Generally speaking, however, these were the only expenses a patient might have to face; his food, shelter and care were free.

Most of the charitable hospitals were well run, and abuses were less than has sometimes been suggested. The nurses of the day generally lived with the patients in the wards, and maintained order and cleanliness. At times of crisis, the Sisters were allowed to hire extra help, women who were paid 1s. a night. If nurses sometimes got a bad name, it was more often from the occasionals than the regular ones. The governing bodies of the hospitals took care to see that affairs were kept in order; a report to the Governors of St. Bartholomew's Hospital in July 1747 reads, "There being no complaint made of any [misconduct] of the Sisters or Nurses of this hospital, your Committee is of opinion that the Sisters and Nurses have done their duty."

Quacks and Mountebanks

Left The quack or stage doctor, whose "surgery" was a platform at a fair.
Right "Bathing in earth, a new way to preserving health and beauty,"
hopefully prescribed by Dr. James Graham

The eighteenth century was a great time for the quack doctor, or mountebank. He boldly claimed he could cure everything, sometimes with a medicine diet (such as stewed prunes and water), or a "specific," such as Dr. John Hill's concoction of dock, sage and valerian. The learned Bishop Berkeley recommended tar-water as a general remedy. Here are four famous quacks:

DOCTOR GRAHAM. James Graham made his first appearance in 1780, taking a house on the Adelphi Terrace, London, adorning it with a large pagan gilt sun, and furnishing the interior with splendour; he had "a commanding figure, an imposing manner, a persuasive voice." But he was a fraud. Every night, he gave public lectures on "How to Restore Health and Vigour by Means of Electricity." Crowds of people attended, paying two guineas each. At the end of the lecture, a naked girl appeared, announced as the Goddess of Health. Graham became famous, and rich. He moved to a larger house in Pall Mall. Unfortunately, he found attendances dropping and had to keep lowering the admission fee. But he had a new stunt, the "Celestial Bed," which stood on four glass legs, and "by means of which the most perfect children could be begotten." It is said he charged £500 per night for its use. He also sold bottles of his "Elixir of Life." But public interest fell, and he then took up lecturing on "bathing in earth," delivering his lectures side by side with the Goddess of Health, both up to the chin in earth. Then his Goddess left him, his creditors pursued him, and he fled to the country. He died in Edinburgh in 1794.

DOCTOR BRODUM. Originally a valet, Brodum learned medical jargon from his master and set up in business himself, selling dozens of bottles of his "Nervous Cordial" and "Botanical Syrup," and later, "Tea for Prolonging Life." He also wrote a book, *Guide to Old Age*.

DOCTOR SOLOMON OF LIVERPOOL. His book, *Guide to Health*, gave fraudulent advice which led to the deaths of many people. His bottles of "Cordial Balm" added to the death toll.

Doctor FREDERICK, Lately come from *Germany*.

BEGS leave to acquaint the Publick, that he undertakes to Cure the Gout, and Rheumatism, without any return; being the firft perfon that ever could Cure the Gout in *London*; Likewife, Cures the yellow Jaundice, Stitching in the Side. He likewife Cures any Body who is bit by a Mad Dog: Gentlemen and Ladies, I call myfelf Mafter; in a Word if you will make Trial where the Public may find great Benefit. No Cure no Pay.

Direct to me at Mr. *Compton's*, the *Crown* and *Feathers*; in *Holbourn*, near *Red Lyon Street*, LONDON.

Advertisement for the famous Dr. Frederick and his incredible cures. The large number of quacks shows how easily people were deceived

MR BUZAGLO OF ITALY. Buzaglo's device was the "Metallic Tractors," two pieces of scrap-metal drawn slowly over afflicted parts of the body, which sufferers of gout and rheumatism foolishly paid five guineas each to buy.

Here is a contemporary description of a quack (1780): he invents "the names of diseases without book, and a bead roll of rattling terms of art which he desires only to remember, not to understand. . . . Thus when people acquaint him with their ills, he tells them 'tis a 'scorbutick [plague], caused by a defluxion from the *os sacrum* afflicting the diaphragm and criocary thenoidal muscles' . . . with which the poor souls are abundantly satisfied, and wonder he should hit upon their distemper so exactly."

The mountebank claimed cures for all diseases

6 The Criminal Classes

C. P. MORITZ thought there were three grades of English criminal: "The cream of criminal society are the pickpockets, who are to be found everywhere – even in the best company – often clean and well-dressed, so that they may be mistaken for people of some standing. In fact, they may actually be so, for there are men who have fallen into want by reason of extravagance and are reduced to this way of living. After them in order of rank come the highwaymen, who ride on horseback, and often, in their desire to relieve the [victim] of his purse put him in terror with an unloaded pistol. But such men have been known to return part of their plunder to a victim gravely distressed, and in any event, they do not murder lightly. Then comes the third, the lowest and vilest class of criminal, the footpads. Tragic examples may be read almost daily in English newspapers of poor people met on the road who have been brutally murdered for a few shillings. These thieves probably murder because they are unable to take flight like the highwayman on his horse, and so, should anyone live to give information concerning them, they can be pretty easily overtaken by a hue-and-cry."

Above Pickpockets were many and double robbery an old trick. *Below* The Poultry Compter, a debtors' prison in London

In Prison

An offender, or suspected offender, was sent to prison to await trial. Almost as soon as the prison gates had clanged shut, the unfortunate prisoner would be called upon by the other prisoners to pay "garnish," a kind of admission fee extorted from him for the benefit of the others. At Horsham, the garnish was 6*s*. 6*d*., at Newgate 2*s*. 6*d*. "Pay or strip" was the rule, and a prisoner who could not pay would often suddenly find himself without any clothes. Innocent or guilty, prisoners usually had to wait a long time for "jail delivery," that is, to be brought out of jail for trial. Assizes in some counties only took place once a year. In the 1770s, Hull only held assizes every three years, and earlier in the century assizes took place up to seven years apart. It is hardly surprising that many prisoners died awaiting trial.

The first type of prison was the "common jail." This included the big county jails under the High Sheriffs, the city jails run by the Corporations, and various private jails of the Church or of rich landowners. The second type was the "Bridewell" which existed all over the country.

Opposite London prisons, *top* Bridewell, *far left* the inner court at Newgate, and *left* the Fleet

These were houses of correction, at first set up under the Poor Law to give work to the vagabonds and beggars; but by the 1750s they were used in much the same way as common jails. Technically, the Bridewells were run by local Justices of the Peace, but in practice they were run by brutal and corrupt jailers, much as the common jails.

There were usually three parts to the big county jails: sleeping-quarters (individual or shared, sometimes little more than dismal dungeons), a day-room for all the prisoners, and a yard for exercise. Beds were almost unknown, and straw a luxury; it was common to chain prisoners to the wall, although women were generally spared this towards the end of the century. At Lincoln Prison, as elsewhere, jailers could make money by releasing prisoners from their chains. The charge for this at Lincoln for a common felon was 2s. 6d. a week, but "a gentleman or better sort of criminal" was expected to pay 5s. Women and men usually slept separately, but shared day-rooms and yards; prisoners were locked up at night. During the day, prison life was dirty and debauched, and lacked any supervision. Dr. Johnson summed it up, "The lewd inflame the lewd, the audacious harden the audacious." Windows were often lacking, not particularly out of cruelty, but because the jailers would have to pay window tax.

Food varied from one prison to another, but it was never enough. In fact, prisoners awaiting trial had no legal claim to any food at all, although in many places they received the "county allowance," originally confined to convicted felons. It usually consisted of a penny-worth of bread (the amount of bread depended on changing prices). But John Howard (1726–89), the prison reformer, noted in 1782 that the penny allowance only bought about eight ounces of bread, barely enough for half a meal a day. Unfortunate debtors were sometimes helped out by sympathetic relatives and other visitors, but felons usually had to manage as best they could.

In the crowded, dirty conditions of prisons, "putrid fevers" were common, and took a large death toll. These fevers, not identified at the time, in fact included typhus and smallpox. Dr. Johnson claimed that "all the complicated horrors of a prison put an end every year to the life of one in four of those that are shut up from the common comforts of human life." The worst case of jail fever of the time took place in May 1750, at the aptly named "Black Sessions." A hundred Newgate prisoners had come for trial to the Old Bailey. As a result of the infections they spread in the court, four of the six judges died, plus forty jurymen and minor officials. People were terrified. In future, Newgate prisoners had to be purified by being washed from head to foot in vinegar, before being exposed to the public. Commenting on conditions at Newgate, the *Gentleman's Magazine* noted, "It is well known how nasty both this and all the rest are kept." John Howard campaigned vigorously for reforms in prison conditions, and helped by Mr. Popham, M.P. for Taunton, persuaded Parliament to pass the Gaol Distemper Act of 1774. Justices were ordered to clean, whitewash and ventilate the prisons under their control, to provide hot and cold baths, to try not to keep prisoners underground, to have a sick-room and prison doctors. But most Justices ignored the Act and there was no one to do anything about it.

A court of sessions in progress

On Trial

When at last the assizes were held in the town of the prison, the prisoners were "delivered" for trial. Often the court lay ten or fifteen miles away, and the prisoners would be forced to march there, heavily chained together. They were then herded together in some dark place to await their turn to be called. Because of the lack of space and conveniences, noted Howard, "this occasions such confusion and distress, and such shrieks and outcries, as can better be conceived than described." Discharged or acquitted prisoners until 1774 usually had to pay jailer's or sheriff's fees; many could not pay, and so found themselves back in prison as debtors. It was a vicious circle.

The legal system had hardly changed in centuries, except that lawyers and judges had invented many new procedures and "legal fictions" to speed up work and reduce injustice. The three Common Law Courts were the King's Bench (crimes, breaches of the peace), Common Pleas (disputes between citizens), and Exchequer (debts owed to the Crown). Each had a jury until 1730; all legal papers were in Latin; delays were long and costly for litigants; full legal term in London only lasted for twelve weeks a year, as many of the judges spent the rest of the time riding around the country on circuit, holding the local assizes, in the county towns.

A visit to a lawyer involved high fees, the progress of justice was slow,
bribery and corruption commonplace

The legal profession at this time was not in good repute. Lawyers' fees
were high, and their work often slow and long drawn out. Boswell once
asked Johnson about this. Did he not "think that the practice of the law,
in some degree, hurt the nice feeling of honesty. Johnson: 'Why no,
Sir, if you act properly. You are not to deceive your clients with false
representations of your opinion: you are not to tell lies to a judge.'
Boswell: 'But what do you think of supporting a cause which you know
to be bad?' Johnson: 'Sir, you do not know it to be good or bad till the
Judge determines it . . .' Boswell: 'But, Sir, does not affecting a warmth
when you have no warmth, and appearing to be clearly of one opinion
when you are in reality of another opinion, does not such dissimulation
impair one's honesty? Is there not some danger that a lawyer may put on
the same mask in common life, in the intercourse with his friends?'
"Johnson: 'Why, no Sir. Everybody knows you are paid for affecting
warmth for your client; and it is, therefore, properly no dissimulation:
the moment you come from the bar you resume your usual [manner]. Sir,
a man will no more carry the artifice of the bar into the common intercourse of society, than a man who is paid for tumbling on his hands will

Above The judges: an exaggerated view perhaps, but this popular picture of the law lords was not without some truth. *Below* The poacher in his hide-out. *Below right* The pillory was still a usual form of public punishment

continue to tumble upon his hands when he should walk upon his feet.'"

Most prisoners were too poor to afford legal help; even if they could their counsel was only allowed to speak on a point of law, and then only if the prisoner himself mentioned it. Everything worked against him; he had probably sweated in prison for months awaiting trial; he was not allowed to see the evidence against him beforehand; and he was, amazingly, not allowed to give evidence himself! Some prisoners "stood mute," that is, refused to answer "guilty" or "not guilty." These unfortunates were stretched out on the ground, pressed with heavy lead weights, and if they still refused to speak, they sometimes died, as happened with one prisoner in 1726. Until 1826, the penalty for all felonies (thefts and robberies as well as murder) was death, unless the prisoner pleaded "benefit of clergy." This was a medieval protection given to clerks, but in fact available to anyone with a smattering of education who could read a passage from a Bible in the dock.

A local criminal court was very different from the same court today, since the magistrate acted more as public prosecutor and chief detective than judge. If the prisoner were sent for trial at assizes, the magistrate would often be the chief witness. Eighteenth-century London had paid magistrates, including the famous "blind beak" Henry Fielding.

Penalties

Transportation was first used as a punishment in 1718, when criminals were deported to Maryland and Virginia in the American Colonies. After working their sentences there, some became settlers, though others found their way home. The American War of Independence (1775–83), however, ended this, and the convicts were confined to the hulks or to houses of correction. But in 1787 transportation was renewed, this time to the infant colony of New South Wales, Australia, and to Norfolk Island. Compared with other forms of punishment in the century, transportation at least served a useful purpose in putting convicts to work on sugar, cotton or tea plantations, although the treatment they received was often cruel. They may have been envied by many debtors thrown into Newgate Prison for life, unable to pay debts of a few shillings.

Branding was a punishment carried out publicly for non-capital offences; it lasted until nearly the end of the eighteenth century. Like all other punishments, it hardly acted as a deterrent, though it did at least put honest citizens on their guard against the branded man. Very often, however, the convict was able to bribe the brander to use a cold iron, and this is probably the main reason why the practice was discontinued.

Whipping, either in private or public, was the most common punishment in towns and villages, the victim usually being tied to a cart and run through the streets in the process. Throughout the ages, whipping or flogging has been greatly feared by hardened criminals. Whipping of prostitutes took place throughout the eighteenth century, as Fielding in his *Coffee House Politician* says, "If you are not a woman of virtue, you will be whipped," and in his *Grub Street Opera*, "Smaller misses for their kisses are in Bridewell banged" – stripped to the waist and in public. Flogging of women was abolished in 1820, although it was still kept for

"Crime's punishment:" a criminal's hand is clamped and branded with an iron hot from the specially portable fire

Opposite Thieving Lane, a notorious street in Westminster, along which criminals were taken to a near-by penitentiary

Above Flogging outside the Old Bailey in London

Above Small offences were sometimes punished by the pillory. *Below* This gruesome invitation to the execution of the informer Jonathan Wild was a warning to other criminals

men. The floggings ordered at the Old Bailey were carried out at Newgate, where the malefactor stood in a small semicircular pew stripped to the waist, his hands held above his head.

The pillory was less popular in the eighteenth century than it had been in earlier times, though it was still sometimes used for minor offenders – rogues and cheats. When the criminal was fiercely hated or feared, the pillory could sometimes be as fatal as the gallows, and a far more terrible ordeal. Titus Oates was taken down from his pillory on the first day nearly dead; in 1763 a man was killed at Bow while in the pillory, and in 1780 another was stoned to death. The pillory was abolished in 1837.

Tyburn Tree

Broadly speaking, crimes in the eighteenth century were either "felonies," or less serious, "misdemeanours." Felonies were punishable by hanging, and since felonies included nearly every form of theft and violence, it is not surprising to find the saying "as well be hung for a sheep as a lamb." Nor was there any general age bar: many teenagers were hanged during the eighteenth century for quite small thefts. But since, without a police force, it was almost impossible to enforce the law, barbarous sentences seemed to be the only answer.

For generations, Tyburn Tree at Marble Arch, London, was the scene of public hangings. Many accounts have survived of "the march to Tyburn." Owing to the fact that death sentences were often lifted or delayed, it seems that Tyburn held less terror for condemned prisoners in Newgate and elsewhere than one might imagine. Condemned prisoners lived freely with the other prisoners, and were not treated much differently. Monday was the usual execution day, and on Sunday evening a service was held in the prison chapel for the condemned, who used it as an excuse to show off their carelessness and recklessness to the delight and amusement of other prisoners and the public. On Monday morning, after taking leave of relatives, the Sheriffs of London or their deputies led the procession of carts, in which the prisoners sat by their coffins, with the Chaplain intoning prayers. The procession usually lasted about half an hour, and was followed by large crowds of onlookers, jeering and cheering, pickpockets, ballad-sellers, preachers, and people brawling.

Fielding gives an account of one such Monday morning: "The day appointed by law for the thief's shame is the day of glory in his own opinion and that of his friends. His procession to Tyburn and his last moments there are all triumphant, attended with the compassion of the meek and tender-hearted, and with the applause, admiration and envy of all the bold and hardened. His [conduct] in his present condition (not the crime, how atrocious soever, which brought him to it) is the subject of universal contemplation."

Someone else described the shouting mob: "It is incredible what a scene of confusion all this often makes, which yet grows worse near the Gallows; and the violent efforts of the most sturdy and resolute of the Mob on the one side, and the potent endeavours of rugged Sheriffs' officers, constables and headboroughs to beat them off on the other; the

Tyburn pictured by Hogarth just before an execution: the prisoner arrives
in a cart standing by his coffin, excitement mounts in the stands from which
the rich watch, and in the jostling crowd below

terrible blows that are struck, the pieces of swinging sticks and blood that
fly about . . . are beyond imagination." And at the end, when the carts
are drawn away, and the prisoners left to choke to death for perhaps
twenty minutes, "the ordinary and executioner, having performed their
duties with small ceremony and concern, seem to be tired and glad it is
over."

Boswell once mentioned to Dr. Johnson "that I had seen the execution
of several convicts at Tyburn, two days before, and that none of them
seemed to be under any concern. Johnson: 'But most of them, Sir, have
never thought at all.' Boswell: 'But is not the fear of death natural to
man?' Johnson: 'So much so, Sir, that the whole of life is but keeping
away the thoughts of it.'"

In 1783 the unpleasant Tyburn procession was abolished, and
executions were held just outside Newgate Prison. A large crowd still
gathered, but there were no carts, no stunts, no special ceremonies. At the
first of these new-style executions, the crowd shuffled away feeling
rather uneasy. Dr. Johnson grumbled, "The public was gratified by a
procession, the criminal was supported by it. Why is all this to be swept
away?" In 1854 public executions were finally abolished.

The condemned cell in Newgate Prison

Debtors

In an age virtually without police, the machinery of law was correspond-
ingly barbarous. But no one suffered more injustices than the debtor.
Daniel Defoe pointed out: "Kings show mercy to traitors, to murderers,

In the yard of Fleet Prison, a new arrival is asked for his "garnish"

Bambridge, a deputy-warden of the Fleet Prison noted for his cruelty

A debtor's family waylay and petition a creditor to forgo the debt

and thieves; and general pardons are often passed to deliver criminals of the worst kinds, and give them an opportunity to retrieve their characters, and show themselves honest for the future; but in debt – we are lost for this world! We cannot obtain the [chance] of being hanged or transported, but our lives must linger within the walls till released by the grave."

Once imprisoned for debt, the debtor could only go free by paying his debts. Yet, shut up from the world, he had no ways of earning money; he could not keep his wife and children, who might eventually desert him or be forced to live with him inside the prison; being in jail cost money: bribes and payments to jailers and turnkeys for food, drink or some privacy. To be locked up for debt was often to lose all hope, and debtors' prisons, such as the Fleet, Ludgate Prison, and the Poultry and Wood Street Compters (used by the Sheriffs of the City of London) had an unrivalled reputation for vice, violence, filth and disorder of all kinds. The appalling state of the law on debts provoked all kinds of abuses, such as unfaithful husbands swearing that their wives owed them money so as to have them clapped in jail. Or, if a debtor was only a few days late in repayment he might be quite unable to pay huge legal fees resulting from a suit, even though he could repay the loan itself.

In 1776 Parliament passed an Act for the Relief of Insolvent Debtors, which reduced the numbers of prisoners by freeing all those who owed more than £1,000 to one man, or who had been arrested before 1776; but the victims had to make a complete list of their possessions, and agree to repay their debts should they receive any inheritance. A private society was set up to help people innocently trapped by small debts. In

1778, for example, they paid the debts of 218 prisoners, who owed on average thirty shillings each – for which they otherwise faced life imprisonment. But major reforms did not come until the nineteenth century.

The Duel

The custom of settling arguments by swords or pistols lasted throughout the century, and indeed beyond (the last fatal duel took place in 1845 when Lieutenant Seton was killed by Lieutenant Hawkey). Although many people disapproved of duelling, others said it encouraged good manners: gentlemen were more ready to bow, raise their hats, and make polite conversation, than risk an argument which might lead to pistols or swords for two at dawn. Perhaps the risk of the duel helps explain the fairly good manners on the roads, crowded as they were with horses, carriages and carts of all kinds, jostling for space on uneven and dangerous surfaces. More than one person noted the politeness and good manners in London, compared with Paris, for example, where brawls were commoner.

On the other hand, duelling did encourage the bully. "Fighting Captain Fitzgerald," for example, terrorized the Committee of Boodle's Club into electing him after he had been blackballed; he made it known that every Committee member would have to fight him if he was blackballed again. Fitzgerald gained an unpleasant reputation in other parts of the country too, including Bath and Tunbridge Wells, where he terrorized heiresses and the brothers who were forced to their defence. In the case of men like this, duelling was discreditable and dangerous.

Every politician had to be ready if necessary to duel, especially on questions of patriotism or national defence which touched everyone's pride. When John Wilkes, the radical, published his celebrated article in issue 45 of *The North Briton*, he risked not only prosecution by the Government but the duel as well. Indeed, he had to duel twice on account of this, first with Lord Talbot, and then with the Secretary of the Treasury, Mr. Maston, who in the way of gentlemen of the day handed over his formal insult, and brought Wilkes to duel in Hyde Park. Many other political duels were fought. Pitt went out with Mr Tierney for accusing him of putting the defences of the country in danger; Fox fought Adam of the War Office, whom he had criticized on the question of Army gunpowder supplies. The most famous political duel was that between Castlereagh and Canning early in the nineteenth century.

Apparently, it was not thought wrong for clergymen to fight duels; they had the same rights and privileges as any other gentleman. One clergyman was killed in a duel with an Army officer; another is said to have been created a baronet and made a dean, even though he had fought three duels; and a third clergyman killed his opponent, without, it seems, receiving any censure from the Church.

A famous duel was fought between Lord Byron (great-uncle of the poet) and Mr. Chaworth at the Star and Garter Tavern, Pall Mall, after an exchange of words with others present (1765): "Lord Byron now came out, and found Mr. Chaworth still on the stairs; it is doubtful

A sword duel at Gresham College

"The Duellists:" the merest trifle was good enough excuse for a duel,
despite inequality of weapons

whether his lordship called upon Mr. Chaworth or Mr. Chaworth called
upon Lord Byron; but both went down to the first landing-place – having
dined upon the second floor – and both called a waiter to show an empty
room, which the waiter did, having first opened the door, and placed a
small tallow-candle, which he had in his hand, on the table; he then
retired, when the gentlemen entered and shut the door after them.

"In a few minutes the affair was decided; the bell was rung, but by
whom is uncertain; the waiter went up, and perceiving what had happened, ran down very frightened, told his master of the catastrophe,
when he ran up to the room, and found the two antagonists standing
close together; Mr. Chaworth had his sword in his left hand, and Lord
Byron his sword in his right; Lord Byron's left hand was round Mr.
Chaworth, and Mr. Chaworth's right hand was round Lord Byron's
neck, and over his shoulder. Mr. Chaworth desired Mr. Fynmore, the
landlord, to take his sword, and Lord Byron delivered up his sword at
the same moment; a surgeon was sent for and came immediately. In the
meantime, six of the company entered the room; when Mr. Chaworth
said that he could not live many hours, that he forgave Lord Byron, and
hoped the world would; that the affair had passed in the dark, only a
small tallow-candle burning in the room; that Lord Byron asked him, if
he addressed the observation on the game to Sir Charles Sedley or to him;
to which he replied, 'If you have anything to say, we had better shut the
door'; that while he was doing this, Lord Byron bid him draw, and in

turning he saw his lordship's sword half-drawn, on which he whipped out his own sword and made the first pass; that the sword being through my lord's waistcoat, he thought that he had killed him; and, asking whether he was not mortally wounded, Lord Byron, while he was speaking, shortened his sword and stabbed him in the belly" (*The Book of Days*).

Dr. Johnson saw nothing against duelling. Boswell thought he "put his argument upon what I have ever thought the most solid basis; that if publick war be allowed to be consistent with morality, private war must be equally so. Indeed, we may observe what strained arguments are used, to reconcile war with the Christian religion. But in my opinion it is exceedingly clear that duelling, having better reasons for its barbarous violence, is more justifiable then than war, in which thousands go forth without any cause of personal quarrel, and massacre each other." This argument may seem strange to us when it is considered wrong to take the law into one's own hands. But one has to remember the almost complete lack of police at this time, and the inability to enforce the law.

7 *The Armed Forces*

Above Marlborough, a great general and ancestor of Sir Winston Churchill. *Below* The French army after their rout at Blenheim

Below "Malborouk" from a French satirical print of Marlborough

Marlborough's Army

When William III died in 1702, French military power dominated Europe; but under the great soldier Marlborough, the British redcoats rose to their highest reputation. After the Battle of Schellenberg (2 July 1704), Louis XIV warned his generals to watch any part of the English line where the redcoats were stationed. But by the time of the Peace of Utrecht (1713), and the downfall of Marlborough, the people of England had raised their old cry against a standing army louder than ever. No one (except the Government) wanted a standing army: the Royalists and Tories remembered the power of Cromwell's Model Army; the Whigs remembered the personal kingship of James II, backed with military force.

During these years, everyone ran down the Army. Parliament refused money to build barracks, and the Army therefore had to be scattered about the country, lodged in alehouses of small towns and villages; each regiment was broken up into six or eight detachments. Local people bombarded the Secretary of War with petitions, demanding the end of this nuisance and burden; country and borough Members of Parliament made lengthy speeches about it. Local magistrates, who were often local landowners, persecuted the idle soldiers with their official powers. This wretched atmosphere, added to the Army being dispersed, led to a new low in discipline and training. Officers who were inactive and on half-pay might have to ride hundreds of miles to inspect all their men. Young officers kicked against the traces; there was no end to drunkenness, brawling, victimization and hooliganism. Perhaps the main reason was that in those days the Army alone stood between public order and disorder; there were no proper police then. Soldiers often found themselves caught in a cross-fire: if they disobeyed their officers, they might be shot for mutiny; if they disobeyed local magistrates, they might be clapped in jail.

The Colonial garrisons in the early eighteenth century were few – Gibraltar, Minorca, New York, Nova Scotia, Jamaica, and a few of the Antilles; and of course the garrisons in Ireland. Administration was appalling; the garrisons often lacked fuel, shelter, adequate food-supplies; in Gibraltar, for instance, huts were provided, but incredible

Opposite Officers and men of the renowned English "redcoats"

Welsh trooper from a cartoon of 1750

though it sounds, the troops were forced to burn them to make fires in the winter. Cheap wine and rum were the main compensations, and greedily welcomed. In Nova Scotia, however, there was not a drop of liquor to be had, and the officers resorted to making a rather nasty "spruce beer." Inactivity led to boredom, laxness and desertion; one West Indies garrison was not relieved for sixty years. Drunkenness and brawling became pastimes, and again and again officers and soldiers lost their lives in duels or simple fist fights. The lash was supposed to maintain discipline, although some soldiers seem to have become hardened to it. One drummer proudly boasted he had received 26,000 lashes in fourteen years, and his officers confirmed that he had certainly received 4,000 between 1727 and 1728, "and yet the man is hearty and well, and in no ways concerned." Some men took lashes for bets.

In the peace (1714–39) both cavalry and infantry wore three-cornered hats, scarlet coats and wide facings; the cavalry wore boots, while the infantry wore scarlet or blue breeches and white gaiters, and carried a musket. Examples of these uniforms can be seen in Hogarth's engraving, *The March to Finchley*, of the time of George II.

The middle and later part of the eighteenth century saw almost continuous warfare involving England around the world – the Austrian

"The March to Finchley," Hogarth's engraving shows the uniforms of cavalry and infantry in peacetime

Succession War, the Seven Years War, the American War of Independence (1775–83) and the Wars of the French Revolution and Napoleon
(1789–1815). The War of the Austrian Succession exposed the many
defects in Army organization, discipline, recruiting and training. But
the chance of fighting and booty gave new life to the troops. The
conditions of active service, however, proved very poor. For sea transport
to America, "he was packed into a hired transport, probably some old
bluff-bowed brig or barque not exceeding two hundred tons in burthen,
and packed so tightly that he could hardly move unless half at least of
his comrades were on deck. He was hustled and bullied by the captain
and the crew for being, quite innocently, in the way in fair weather;
and in foul he was battened down below decks, miserably seasick and
frightened out of his life. His food was chiefly salt pork, very likely
mouldy, and certainly ill-cooked, eked out with biscuits full of weevils . . .
it was extremely doubtful when, if ever, he would arrive at his destina-
tion." It might take six or eight months or more to reach the New World.
Even if he survived the hardship of the journey, and possibly a campaign
in an unhealthy climate, there was little to celebrate. The soldier in the
eighteenth century was never thought of as a hero.

William Pitt, Paymaster of the
Forces

Pitt's Militia

The idea of a national militia belonged to William Pitt (1708–78).

Lance drill, an illustration from the handbook of the City of London Militia

The militia was a military force raised by ballot throughout the land,
and intended for home defence, so as to free the whole of the regular
army for campaigns overseas. Everyone chosen by the ballot had to
serve for three years. After initial opposition, the Bill became law in
1757, enabling Pitt to turn the tide of the war in North America. The
ballot was not very well organized, and was open to all the abuses of
patronage and corruption that eighteenth-century society could offer;
it produced a very motley standard of troops.

   Not very much is known in detail of militia service, although Boswell
(1740–95) tells us that Johnson (1709–84) "was once drawn to serve in

Below Medal struck after the
Battle of Dettingen, the last
where an English king led his
troops in person

Army recruiting normally depended on volunteers, with dubious success

Little respect was shown to London's militia, the Trained Bands

the militia, the Trained Bands of the City of London . . . It may be believed he did not serve in person." (It was always possible, with friends in the right places, to arrange for someone to take your place.) But Johnson did, however, equip himself with the necessary musket, sword and leather belt. Another literary figure, Edward Gibbon (1737–94) served, and records that his regiment was efficient, although when he had learned his duties he found it very boring. Much of the time there was nothing to do except gossip with his fellow militiamen. Most militia regiments were very casual, at least at the start; drunkenness was rife, parades were lax, and drill often non-existent. Discipline was improved, however, when the militia regiments were made to share quarters with the regular regiments, being put under the same orders; the discipline of the sergeants improved too. After basic training, live ammunition was issued to the militiamen, who soon used up large quantities of it in shooting-matches, and hunting hares and foxes in the surrounding countryside.

The Press Gang

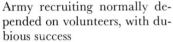

Press-gang victim parted from his wife

The age-old source of recruiting for the Royal Navy was the seafaring population – fishermen, lightermen, merchant seamen. These were usually volunteers, but when recruiting was low, or the demands of war were high, resort was made to the press-gang. The trouble was that, in peacetime, there were about 16,000 sailors, whereas during wartime 80,000 were needed, five times the number. Lord Mansfield, the lawyer, justified press-ganging as "founded upon immemorial usage allowed for ages. If not, it can have no ground to stand on. The practice is deduced

Left The Press-Gang at work. *Middle* The idle sailor, a gibe at Walpole's
pacific policy. *Right* The ship's cook, sketched by Rowlandson

from that trite maxim of the constitutional law of England that private
mischief had better be submitted to, than public detriment should
ensue."

The Royal Navy was hardly an endearing employer. Wages were
lower than in merchant ships; discipline – the lash and keel-hauling –
was more brutal; spells ashore were shorter; and the chance for booty or
plunder was less than on merchant privateers. When a fleet was fitting
out, recruits were offered a bounty of £2, plus two months' wages in
advance, plus conduct money. But this never attracted enough people,
although some took advantage of it: John Hodgson for example, between
the ages of twenty and twenty-six enlisted and deserted so many times
that he collected over £600 in bounty money; but he endured many
floggings for desertion, and was finally hung at Tyburn.

"To press" in the eighteenth century meant "to force." When
recruiting went badly, press-gangs of half a dozen sailors, armed with a
press-warrant, would lie in wait for vagabonds, passers-by, foreigners,
merchant seamen going home and clap them into service, taking them by
force if necessary. Admiral Vernon, unjustly removed from the Navy
because of his outspokenness, said the fleet was "manned by violence,
and maintained by cruelty." Once men were press-ganged, he added,
they were "in effect condemned to death, since they are never allowed
again to set foot on shore, but turned over from ship to ship." Impressed
men would do almost anything to escape. The captain of a sloop in 1743
reported that four men recently impressed "swam away from the ship in
the night when it blowed so hard that a boat could not row ahead," and
although two others had drowned in the attempt shortly before.

C. P. Moritz in 1782 wrote, "A foreigner has nothing to fear from the

A sailor and his girl

Press Gang here provided he keeps away from suspicious places. Standing on dry land on Tower Hill . . . is a ship . . . This is no more than an ingenious device for catching unwary visitors. Simple people who stand and stare at it – some of whom come from the country districts – are approached by a man who offers for a trifle to show them round the ship . . . as soon as they are aboard they are trapped and, according to their circumstances, are either released or pressed for service as sailors."

Sailors

As soon as the sailor, press-ganged or volunteer, arrived on board his ship, he was given a ticket for his pay. This ticket recorded the date he joined, the amount of his pay, and was signed by the Captain, Purser, Master and Bo'sun. When the voyage was completed, he handed in his ticket and received his pay. No payments were made during a voyage. An ordinary seaman got 19s. a month, but 24s. a month was earned by able seamen, the midshipman ordinary, cooks, swabbers, coopers, the Captain's cook, and the trumpeter.

The scale of food laid down in 1745 was bad, scanty and monotonous:

	Biscuits lb.	Beer gal.	Beef lb.	Pork lb.	Pease pts.	Oat-meal pts.	Butter oz.	Cheese oz.
Sunday	1	1		1	$\frac{1}{2}$			
Monday	1	1				1	2	4
Tuesday	1	1	2					
Wednesday	1	1			$\frac{1}{2}$	1	2	4
Thursday	1	1		1	$\frac{1}{2}$			
Friday	1	1			$\frac{1}{2}$	1	2	4
Saturday	1	1	2					

Fresh meat was only given two days a week, even in port. Complaints were frequent, but naval administrators ignored them. Cruising off Brest in 1759, Hawke wrote to the Quartermaster at Plymouth: "The beer brewed at your port is so excessively bad that it employs the whole time of the squadron in surveying it and throwing it overboard . . . a quantity of bread from the *Ramillies* will be returned to you by the *Elizabeth*, though not altogether unfit for use, yet so full of weevils and maggots that it would have infected all the bread come on board this day."

The trouble was, as this contemporary jingle tells us, in peacetime the Navy hardly bothered even to feed its sailors:

> Ere Hawke did bang
> Monsieur Conflans
> You sent us beef and beer;
> Now Monsieur's beat,
> We've nought to eat,
> Since you have nought to fear!

Captain Avery, the pirate, receiving chests of stolen treasure

Hundreds upon hundreds of sailors died of scurvy, a disease due to lack of vitamin c; its unpleasant symptoms include hair falling out. The reason for scurvy was not understood at the time, although in the last half of the century it was found that lime juice reduced the disease; but lime juice was not officially used until as late as 1795. Admiral Geary thought it rare for a ship to last longer than six weeks before scurvy appeared among the men. Outbreaks of scurvy could be as decisive in a naval campaign as firing power. Naval regulations provided for a "convenient room" (sick-room) for the sick and wounded. But the suffering of these poor people in the tropics could be really horrible. Smollett leaves a terrible picture in *Roderick Random* of such conditions off Cartagena in 1741. Some fleets sailed with hospital ships, staffed with surgeons, but some admirals themselves took an interest in medical matters, not always to the advantage of the patients. One admiral

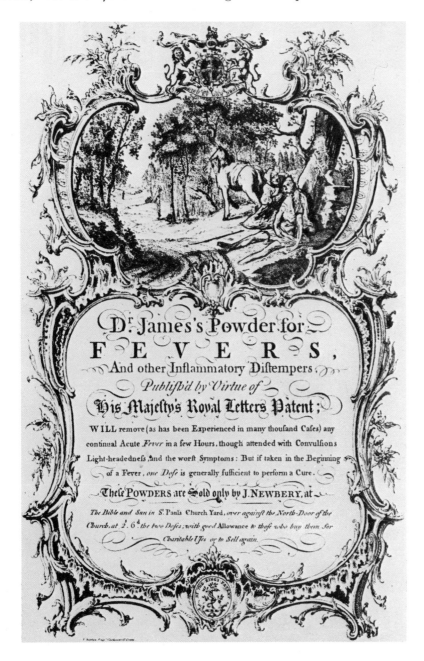

An advertisement for "Doctor James's Powders"

believed firmly in "James' Powders" though "he gave up his favourite nostrum" when it was pointed out to him that it was sending his men to their deaths at the rate of four a day.

The surgeons were not very well qualified, and were only paid £5 a month, £1 more than the boatswain. Out of this they had to buy their own instruments. "If the poor seaman, after being forced on board if he were not a volunteer, after facing the enemy, stomaching the food, and withstanding the climate, survived also the ministrations of the physician and the surgeon, he might in the end get some reward in the form of a gratuity from the chest at Chatham, and possibly a berth in Greenwich Hospital: while if he did not survive, he had the satisfaction of knowing that his widow would be entitled to a year's pay, and that his posthumous children would be deemed orphans!" (Admiral Sir Herbert Richmond.)

Few ordinary seamen became commissioned officers. Those that were rarely rose above rank of lieutenant (Captain Cook was a notable exception). Officers were found in other ways. One was for a boy of thirteen to enter as a Captain's servant, leading eventually to a lieutenantcy; another was to enter from the Naval Academy. Instructions from the Naval Academy, addressed to a ship's Captain in 1742, read: "You are to take care that he applies himself to the duty of a seaman, and he is to have the privilege of walking the quarter deck. You are to allot him a proper place to lie in without setting up any cabin and you are to rate him 'volunteer per order' which will entitle him to able seaman's pay. You are to oblige him to keep a journal, and to draw the appearances of headlands, coasts, bays, sands, rocks and suchlike: and you are to take care that the master, boatswain and schoolmaster do instruct him in all parts of learning that may qualify him to do the duty of able seaman and midshipman. After two years' service at sea, you are to rate him Midshipman ordinary, or midshipman if he shall be qualified for it . . ."

However youngsters entered the navy, they were led on by adults to do so at an early age, usually between twelve and fourteen. Otherwise, they would not easily become used to the hard life, and might give it up. George III wrote: "All the sea officers I have ever consulted as to the proper age for sending young officers to sea concurred in the opinion that fourteen is as late as so hardy a profession can be embraced with the smallest prospect of success." Strictly speaking, midshipmen and mates were not allowed to take commissions until the age of twenty-one, but many lied about their age. Promotion after that was rapid, and many became captains at an early age. It was usual to spend ten, even twenty years in this rank, before family connections or seniority brought promotion to flag rank – with all the prestige, patronage, bounty, and retinues this brought in its wake.

The Royal Naval School at Greenwich outside London

Admiral Nelson did much to improve conditions of naval service

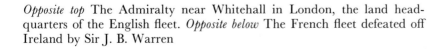

Opposite top The Admiralty near Whitehall in London, the land headquarters of the English fleet. *Opposite below* The French fleet defeated off Ireland by Sir J. B. Warren

8 Religion, Education and the Arts

Priests and Parsons

During the eighteenth century, a great gulf divided the higher and the lower clergy, echoing that between the upper and lower classes. While the Bishop of Winchester, for example, received £5,000 a year, the average curate or country parson – of whom there were 6,000 to 7,000 – received only £30 or £40 a year, which was poverty level even in those days (although these figures doubled by about 1800). In 1730, for example, John Wesley, then a young curate at Stanton Harcourt, received £30 a year. Many curates, however, added to their incomes by working as local schoolmasters. Curates suffered from many other disadvantages: they were often appointed by wealthy patrons, such as a local landlord, and could be sent packing without notice. Many curates also lacked proper accommodation, although some, like Parson Woodforde, were able to lodge with the local squire. Woodforde's terms were, "That I should live as he does (which is very well I am sure), that I should have my Linnen washed by him, and that he should keep my horse (corn excepted) £21;" and for every day Woodforde was away, he received 1s. 1½d. expenses. He was lucky. Other curates added to their income by plurality (holding more than one post at a time), but this only added to the abuse of non-residence. Boswell told Dr. Johnson that curates needed at least £100, but Johnson replied, smugly, that "if no curate were to be permitted unless he had £100 a year, their number would be very small, which would be a disadvantage."

Part of the difficulty in improving the lot of curates and parsons was the medieval character of Church government – for example, bishops were away from their dioceses most of the year, busy in Parliament. With all these problems, recruiting good curates became very difficult; educated and ambitious young men preferred to work as chaplains or canons, finding these jobs through family patronage. As a result, the eighteenth-century Church was in low repute.

C. P. Moritz wrote: "The English clergy, especially in London, are notorious for their free and easy way of life. While I have been living here, one of them has fought a duel in Hyde Park and shot his opponent. He was tried by jury and found guilty of manslaughter, or unpremeditated homicide, for which he was 'branded' on the hand with a *cold* iron, this

Opposite Contemporary views of the clergy. *Top* the curate going on duty and *far left* after work returns to his poor home. *Left* the master parson could afford a good horse for himself

Above John Wesley, the founder of Methodism

Above Caricature of a Jesuit

George Whitefield, another Dissenting preacher

being a privilege the nobility and clergy enjoy over other murderers." Nor was the standard of preaching high. "I have heard," said Moritz, "the most miserable twaddle from the pulpits. Today I have been in several churches where the sermons seem to have been drawn from pamphlets on dogma. It is said there is a Jew living here from whom the clergy order sermons to be written for money."

Dissenters

The older Dissenters – the Unitarians of Richard Price and Joseph Priestley, the Independents and the Quakers – became a major social force in the new industrial towns which grew in the later part of the century. Banned by law from Parliament and the municipal corporations, they worked hard instead as Improvement Commissioners in the towns, pioneering public health, street lighting, education, and building hospitals and asylums. The Wesleyans, unlike other Dissenters, avoided Radicalism, devoting themselves to religious conversion and belief. By hard work and skill, many Dissenters became rich tradesmen and merchants, and used their fortunes and abilities to improve the life of their employees, apprentices and journeymen.

In this lawless age, the town mob was a byword. There were French Revolution riots, No Popery riots, and industrial damage at Arkwright's Nottingham factory and elsewhere. Mass hysteria lay very near the surface. The hell-fire preachers were the ones to arouse it. With the growing irrelevance of Anglican parish boundaries to the new towns, with sharp rises in the cost of bread, and new tensions in those families who were giving up the countryside for mines and factories, rich preaching material lay ready for Wesley, Whitefield and other dynamic speakers. Wesley's *Journal* describes scenes which would astonish modern readers – of sinners overcome with fearful pains when listening to the fiery Gospel, writhing in torment on the ground. Many people at the time, Dissenters included, spoke out against Wesley's methods, which seemed to lack any intellectual message, and to rely purely on emotion. After these early days, Methodism quietened down; "hell-fire" preaching went on in the new chapels, but attempts were now made to educate the people for this world as well as the next.

Johnson was one of those who detested the hell-fire preachers. Boswell wrote, "He would not allow much merit to Whitefield's oratory. 'His popularity, Sir' said he, 'is chiefly owing to the peculiarity of his manner. He would be followed by crowds were he to wear a night-cap in the pulpit, or were he to preach from a tree.'"

At School

During the seventeenth century, great plans had been afoot to improve education, supported by such men as Milton, Locke and Petty, but the will to reform had not survived into the eighteenth century. There still existed many of the great grammar schools of the Middle Ages and Renaissance, and a number of elementary schools were run by religious bodies and guilds; but with an exploding population these were not

"An Awful Warning" or what happens when religion is ignored

adequate, especially for teaching subjects needed in an age of commerce and enterprise – reading, writing and arithmetic. Liberal men, and especially Nonconformists, would have liked to see the Government create a system of primary education, but this was never a real possibility. Instead, there sprang up many small voluntary "dames' schools" in town and country areas; Dr. Johnson attended one at Lichfield. A Government Committee found there were about 50,000 children in these schools by 1816.

A start was made by charitable people in founding small schools up and down the country. A charity school for twenty boys was set up in Lambeth; Dr. Busby paid for the education of poor boys in Westminster, where a Blue-coat School for fifty boys was also founded; together with others, London by 1704 had over fifty such schools, educating over 2,000 children. At the death of George I charity schools could be found in most parts of the country, with about 22,000 boys and 6,000 girls, aged seven to twelve. Addison enthusiastically called these schools "the glory of the age." The main concern was teaching religion, but reading, writing and arithmetic were included, although girls generally studied sewing instead of arithmetic.

Many grammar schools had survived the Reformation, and together with sixteenth-century ones, grew into what was to become the great public school system of the nineteenth century: schools such as Eton, Harrow, Rugby, Winchester, King's School Canterbury, Oundle, Tonbridge. But during the eighteenth century, their standards were low. Chief Justice Kenyon dubbed them "empty walls without scholars." The main subjects taught were Latin and Greek, with some Hebrew.

A parson's school in 1750

University don with wig and gown removed is expelled for insulting a lady

A drunken scholar shocks the university's Vice-Chancellor. These cartoons satirize the low standards of the universities.

Writing and arithmetic were ignored, and Joseph Priestley called their discipline "a common topic of ridicule."

Oxford and Cambridge

At Oxford and Cambridge, the two universities of eighteenth-century England, lethargy reigned. The old medieval and Renaissance forms remained, but the life had gone out of them. University government was regulated by statutes centuries old and by a strongly clerical atmosphere. At Oxford science was virtually ignored, though at Cambridge, Newtonian mathematics was coming to take pride of place over the Classics. Cambridge science was aided by the creation of many new professorships in the first half of the century: chemistry, astronomy, experimental philosophy, anatomy, botany, Arabic, geology, geometry. Although Cambridge had its Jacobites (twenty-two Jacobite Fellows were removed in 1717), the main feeling was Whig, and George II was glad to contribute £2,000 towards the building of the Senate House; but Oxford, with strong Jacobite traditions, still hankered after the Stuart line of kings. The academic leadership of Oxford at this time was poor, although many great men of the period spent their undergraduate days there, including Dr. Johnson, who went up to Pembroke College in 1728.

The method of study was the "disputation," a medieval form of training in which a subject was discussed ("disputed") between the students and a Master. Disputations in grammar and logic took place three days a week in term time, and continued for several terms. C. P. Moritz visited Oxford in 1782 and entered the great hall "where official disputations are held. This is a round building fitted with rows of benches around its walls, each row raised higher than that in front of it; on these, the doctors, masters and undergraduates sit, and in the midst two rostrums are built right opposite to each other, from which the disputants address each other." In the public examination, the candidates for a Bachelor's or Master's degree disputed further, supervized by a Moderator. Subjects included philosophy, history, astronomy and Hebrew. In the first half of the century the examinations were a mockery; students and examiners were often drinking companions. C. P. Moritz noted, "Dons and undergraduates are always dropping into the Mitre for a chat, a pot of ale and a short parley with the landlord's daughter. She is a well-behaved wench." There was little or no difference between a Bachelor's degree and that of a Master; there were no written examinations. But by 1763 Cambridge was holding proper examinations for degrees but a real examination and honours list was not set up at Oxford until 1800.

The standard of teaching was low. Cowper referred to "ignorance in stilts," and Gilbert Wakefield called Cambridge lectures "odious beyond conception." In 1745, Adam Smith, a young student at Balliol, said that most Professors had "given up altogether even the pretence of teaching." But if lecturing was bad, hope lay in the growing tutorial system, despite the "invitations, suppers, wine and fruit" referred to by Wordsworth, and despite the old-fashioned views of men like Dr. Johnson, who said disapprovingly, "Our Universities were founded to bring up members for the Church of England."

Newspapers

The eighteenth century saw many English newspapers grow and flourish. Circulations remained fairly small, however, mainly due to the technical problems of distribution and printing. The first steam-press, for instance, was not in operation until 1814, and newspapers had to be printed on hand-presses which had barely changed since the time of William Caxton. Most newspapers consisted of a single large sheet of paper, printed on both sides, and folded once to make four pages. Each page measured roughly twelve inches by six. Cowper spoke of a newspaper as being "a folio of four pages." In the reign of Queen Anne, each page contained two columns or "rows," but by the end of the century the custom was to have four columns a page, using a larger sheet.

During Walpole's time, the most important newspapers were political. Walpole himself founded the *Daily Gazeteer* (1735) to defend his policies, and between 1731 and 1741, he spent about £5,000 on subsidizing

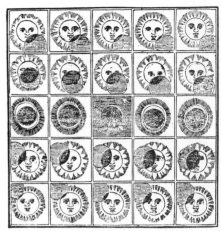

The eclipse of the sun illustrated in the *Weekly Journal* or *British Gazeteer* (1724)

Vendors of some of the many newspapers and journals

newspapers which supported him. Walpole's Court Party was opposed by the Whig Country Party, who had a newspaper of their own, *The Country Journal or The Craftsman*, largely written by Nicholas Amherst, and published weekly. Bolingbroke was its best-known writer. With a circulation topping 12,000, this paper, usually known as *The Craftsman*, was the most talented and popular in the early eighteenth century. Many people criticized the Press. Pulteney spoke of "the contemptible scribblers of the ministerial vindications: a herd of wretches whom neither information can enlighten, nor affluence elevate; low drudges of scurrility . . ." Another political paper was *The Champion* (1739), which featured book reviews, and articles on manners of the time.

Journals were newspapers which came out weekly; they tended to be more reflective, reviewing the week's events, and having less political connexions. They included the anti-Jacobite and satirical *Jacobite's Journal*, and the *Covent Garden Journal* (1752) which had a strong moral tone. *The Westminster Journal* (1741) survived into the next century; *Old England* was another important journal, whose contributors included

Newspaper picture of a fiery apparition in the air, London (1710)

William Guthrie, Chesterfield and Horace Walpole. The *Gentleman's Journal* anticipated the magazine. Journals began to take the place of pamphlets and broadsheets as propaganda organs.

"Advertizers" were newspapers connected mainly with business and commerce. One of the first was the famous *Daily Advertizer* (1731). In the beginning it only contained advertisements, rather like the *Exchange and Mart* today, and gave the prices of stocks and shares. *The Tatler*, though not an "advertizer," sometimes devoted half its space to advertisements. Many papers about trade were mainly political, such as Defoe's *Mercator* and *The British Merchant* (1713). *The Daily Advertizer* went far towards obtaining a monopoly of advertizing. It stated in one issue, "all the Advertisements being collected together, every person may readily find out whatever can properly fall under the Denomination of an Advertisement, without having recourse to any other Paper." The "advertizers," in fact, did much to get businessmen into the habit of advertizing, as the circulation increased. "Advertizers" were morning papers. "Close to the Royal Exchange," wrote Moritz in 1782, "is a little shop where you can read as many of the current newspapers as you wish on payment of a penny or halfpenny. This shop is continuously full; people stand and read hastily for a while, pay their halfpenny, and go."

We have already seen one or two examples of notices which appeared in the "advertizers" (see pages 10 and 67). Until 1772 negroes were often bought and sold in England, and advertisements like this could occasionally be seen:

TO BE SOLD
A Fine Negro Boy
Of about 4 Feet 5 Inches High
Of a Sober, tractable Humane Disposition
Eleven or Twelve years of Age
Talks English very Well
And can Dress Hair in a Tollerable Way

In the 1750s London boasted several evening papers, published three times a week, among them: *The Whitehall Evening Post*, *The London Evening Post* and *The General Evening Post*. The most important, however, was *The London Chronicle* or *Universal Evening Post*. Unlike the others with four pages, this had eight, and was also the first of the "Chronicles"; it also had few advertisements, never more than five of the twenty-four columns. It was the first "family paper," and safe if dull at times. Deaths, Marriages and Preferments were listed in it. *The London Chronicle* started a new fashion in the middle of the eighteenth century for newspaper-reading for a wider public, not always concerned with politics.

With the accession of George III in 1760 and the Ministry of Bute, politics began once more to dominate newspaper space. Most of the new political newspapers formed at this time sought to rid the King of un-popular Ministers, and included *The North Briton* (1762). On 23 April 1763, Wilkes wrote his famous article which led to his prosecution, although the paper itself continued. Others were *The Monitor* (1755), *The Middlesex Journal* (1769), which began as a result of the notorious elections, and *The Morning Chronicle* (1769). In the same year of 1769,

Top Advertisements came with the growth of newspapers. *Middle* Trading a negro slave. *Left* John Wilkes, whose political paper *The North Briton* was prosecuted

The Public Advertizer carried the first of the famous and anonymous "Letters to Junius" whose invective and rhetoric in political causes made them one of the most celebrated literary pieces of the century. To this day, no one knows for certain who "Junius" really was. The most likely writer was perhaps Sir Philip Francis. The growing influence of the Press led to repeated disputes with Governments as to the right or otherwise of reporting Parliamentary matters, and a number of prosecutions took place.

Newspapers appeared in many towns up and down the country for the first time during the eighteenth century:

1701	Norwich	1718	Cirencester, Plymouth, Leeds
1702	Bristol		
1707	Exeter	1719	York, Ludlow, Derby, Manchester
1709	Worcester		
1710	Newcastle, Nottingham	1720	Northampton, Ipswich
1712	Liverpool, Stamford	1721	Chester
1715	Salisbury	1722	Gloucester
1716	Bury St Edmunds, St Ives, Hunts	1723	Reading
1717	Canterbury	1725	Maidstone

Top A writer with quill pen, ink-pot and sand-box. *Bottom* A street vendor selling ink

Letter-writing

Most English people in the eighteenth century could not read or write. Most had no education. The educated middle and upper classes wrote a good many letters and diaries – which leave a clear picture of their life and times. A small tradesman who did not know how to write a letter would ask a friend to do it for him, or if he were desperate he might go to a lawyer's clerk and pay a fee, especially if the letter he wanted to send was an important one. Quill pens were used, sharpened to a point, and with a small split to let the ink run smoothly. The writer kept an ink-well on his desk which he filled by calling upon one of the ink-sellers who sold their wares in the streets. Writing-paper was thick and soft, and the rag content could easily be felt. When the letter had been written, the writer threw a small handful of silver sand across it to dry the ink; this was necessary because the paper was so absorbent, and ink was liable to fuzz.

In the eighteenth century, postage depended on the distance the letter was to be sent. Distances under 80 miles cost 2*d.* or 3*d.*; from 80 to 150 miles cost 5*d.*, and over 150 miles cost 6*d.* There were special charges for some routes: London to Edinburgh was 7*d.*, London to Dublin 6*d.*, London to America 1*s.*, to France 10*d.*, to Spain 1*s.* 6*d.* and so on. A penny post was also operated. John Palmer of Bath was the first to set up a proper mail-coach service. The first coach left from London to Bristol at 8 a.m. on 8 August 1784 with an average speed of seven miles an hour. Overseas mail went by "packet-boat." By 1800, the staff of the Post Office consisted of two Postmaster-Generals, and about 250 clerks and letter-carriers, with salaries from £40 to £140. There were many abuses of the service, especially by Members of Parliament who sold their special pre-franked envelopes to friends and relatives. In 1763, about

seven million franked letters were posted. Major reforms did not occur until the next century, with the work of Rowland Hill. By 1800 postal charges had increased, and many people complained that each separate sheet in the envelope had to be paid for, so that to send one sheet to Edinburgh from London cost 1s. 1½d., while three sheets cost 3s. 4½d.

Music and Musicians

Changing tastes in music depended a good deal on noble and Church patronage, which set a variety of new fashions. In the middle of the century, some composers and players found themselves involved in the dispute between George II and the Prince of Wales, who sought to establish a rival Court of his own at Montagu House. When Handel, for example, wrote an anthem for the Prince's marriage, he paid dearly: George II withdrew his patronage and managed to force Covent Garden into bankruptcy. Like many others, Handel found his fortunes swinging from one extreme to another, in a climate unconducive to serious, steady work.

Opera was the most popular form of music to contemporaries, who were not attuned to listening to "music for music's sake." They demanded a story. As Burney, father of the novelist Fanny Burney, wrote in his *History of Music* (1776): "Now it may be asked, what entertainment there is for the mind in a concerto, sonata or solo? They are objects of mere gratification to the ear . . . however, imagination may divert itself with the idea that a fine *adagio* is a tragical story; an *andante* or *grazioso* an elegant narrative of some tranquil event, an *allegro* a tale of merriment . . ." Like nearly all his contemporaries, Burney preferred opera: "As the Opera includes nearly every species of music, vocal and instrumental, its annals . . . seem nearly to comprise the whole history of the art; for here we have the most varied and impassioned composition, the most refined singing, the completed orchestra . . . choruses and solemn scenes of splendid sacrifice or funeral sorrow." In view of the demand for a story, and for strong singing, it is not surprising that John Gay's *Beggar's Opera*, with its striking tunes and satirical content, should have been such a success with the people, while composers of "pure" music achieved less recognition, and Dr. Johnson could remark sourly, "Pray sir, who is this Bach? Is he a piper?"

This was the age, too, of the harpsichord, as popular then as the piano is today. Songs were popular – especially Dr. Arne's Shakespearian lyrics, "Where the bee sucks," and "Blow, blow thou Winter Wind," Dibdin's "Tom Bowling" and traditional and patriotic songs such as "Admiral Benbow," Arne's "Rule Britannia," Boyce's "Hearts of Oak," and of course the National Anthem, composer unknown.

Johnson's attitude to music was rather ambiguous. But he did once confess a liking for the "fiddle" to Oliver Goldsmith: "There is nothing, I think, in which the power of art is so much shown as in playing on the fiddle. In all other things we can do something *at first*. Any man will forge a bar of iron if you give him a hammer; not so well as a smith, but tolerably. A man will saw a piece of wood, and make a box, though a clumsy one. But give him a fiddle and a fiddle stick and he can do

Top The postman, *second* a scene from "The Beggar's Opera" (1728), *third* Handel, one of the greatest composers of the age, *bottom* Thomas Arne, lawyer and musician, who wrote "Rule Britannia"

nothing." In 1775, Johnson had been involved in an argument against the value and art of music. Yet, "after having spoken slightingly of music, he was observed to listen very attentively while Miss Thrale played on the harpsichord, and with eagerness he called to her, 'Why don't you dash away like Burney?' Dr. Burney upon this said to him, 'I believe, sir, we shall make a musician of you at last.' Johnson with candid complacency replied, 'Sir, I shall be glad to have a new sense given to me.'"

Bookshops and Libraries

Some of the first English bookshops appeared in the eighteenth century, selling books on politics, religion, law, gardening, grammar and natural history. The customers were wealthy and educated. Booksellers bought their stock from large wholesalers or else worked together with an author, who would print his own books and sell them through the bookshop, as well as by private subscription to friends and acquaintances. Some booksellers themselves acted as "publishers," that is, commissioning authors to write books, and having the books printed. In the eighteenth century, books were very expensive, being printed and bound by hand, and sold in editions of only a few hundreds. Pamphlets cost around 1s., novels and essays around 3s. and larger books one or two guineas – large sums at a time when the weekly wages of ordinary people were only measured in shillings and pence.

Above The harpsichord enjoyed great popularity. *Bottom left* The author, Sterne, selling his own books. *Bottom right* Books for sale in *The Idler* (1761)

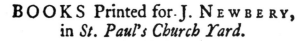

BOOKS Printed for J. NEWBERY, in *St. Paul's Church Yard.*

1. THE RAMBLER. In four Volumes in Twelves. The fifth Edition. Price Twelve Shillings bound.

2. The STUDENT; or the *Oxford* and *Cambridge* Monthly Miscellany. Consisting of Original Essays, in Prose and Verse. In two Volumes Octavo. Price Twelve Shillings.

3. A familiar Explanation of the Poetical Works of MILTON. To which is prefixed Mr ADDISON's Criticism on *Paradise Lost.* With a Preface by the Rev. Mr. *Dodd.* Price Three Shillings bound.

4. The Works of ANACREON, SAPPHO, BION, MOSCHUS, and MUSÆUS. Translated from the original Greek, by *Francis Fawkes,* M. A. Price Three Shillings bound.

5. The SHRUBS of PARNASSUS: Consisting of a Variety of Poetical Essays, moral and comic. By *J. Copywell,* of Lincoln's Inn, Esq; Price Three Shillings bound.

6. The NONPAREIL, or, The Quintessence of Wit and Humour: Being a choice Selection of those Pieces that were most admired in the ever-to-be-remember'd *Midwife,* or *Old Woman's Magazine*; Pieces which, (as a celebrated Author observes) will stand the Test of all Ages, and live and be read till Time is no more. To which is added, an Index to Mankind; or Maxims selected from the Wits of all Nations, for the Benefit of the present Age, and of Posterity. Interspersed with some Axioms in Life, and seasonable Reflections by the same Author. With a PREFACE by her good Friend the late Mr. POPE.

Eighteenth-century libraries, *top left* a large private collection, *top right*
Francis Noble's famous circulating library, *left* Lackington & Allen, another
famous London library and *right* Hall's library at Margate

Circulating libraries first grew up in the eighteenth century; the first
one was opened in 1740 by a bookseller in the Strand, London, called
Batho. Over twenty were in existence by 1800, including Francis
Noble's, and Lackington & Allen's. Customers paid a small fee for the
right to borrow books for reading at home. Outside London, book clubs
were more popular than circulating libraries; a group of people would
get together, pooling perhaps a guinea each, and buy and sell their
own chosen books among themselves. They were usually managed by
ladies, and their success depended on getting people together and finding
plenty of interests in common.

Private libraries, even very small ones were few and far between.
In the eighteenth century, the following was regarded as a very large
selection of books:

The garden front of the British
Museum in London

Bunyan's *Pilgrim's Progress* *Robin Hood's Garland*
Foxe's *Book of Martyrs* *The Seven Champions*
The Whole Duty of Man Turner's *Spectator*
Baker's *Chronicles* *The Tale of a Tub*
The Complete Letter-Writer Culpepper's *Herbal*
Defoe's *Robinson Crusoe*

Few people could afford, or felt the need for more. Hardly any
member of the middle classes owned a single book. Some of the really
large private libraries, such as that of Sir Hans Sloane (42,000 volumes)

eventually formed the nucleus of the British Museum Library, available to scholars. Apart from individuals, other large libraries were owned by public institutions, such as the Gray's Inn Library (law books), and College of Physicians Library (medical books). Since so few people could afford an education, the ownership of books became a mark of great social distinction.

One of the great bibliophiles of the time was, of course, Dr. Johnson, compiler of the *Dictionary*. The young novelist Fanny Burney met him when Johnson came to her father's house, and was upset that he seemed to prefer books to people: "His attention, however, was not diverted five minutes from the books, as we were in the library; he pored over them, shelf by shelf, almost touching the backs of them with his eyelashes as he read their titles. At last, having fixed upon one, he began, without further ceremony, to read (to himself), all the time standing at a distance to the company. We were all very much provoked, as we perfectly languished to hear him talk."

Literacy was growing; books and newspapers were finding a wider public, and ideas were being developed and exchanged more freely than ever before. The improvements in road communications had speeded up the post so far that what happened in London or Bristol was known in every important locality within the next few days. People had only just begun to grasp the great benefits that this would bring to commerce, trade and government, but they saw that much of the corruption and parochialism of the past was doomed. By these means, the English people had gained a firmer hold on their own future, and it only remained to be seen how they would apply it.

Reading a book

"The Distrest Poet" living in his garret

Epilogue

A new craze: cricket for women

The people of eighteenth-century England believed they had attained a new level of civilization. Between 1700 and 1800 the population had doubled, many great newspapers had been founded, the middle classes – merchants and small shopkeepers, doctors, lawyers, the new landowners – had come to feel more sure of their identity. Exotic influences sprang from a growing internationalism, brought about by the Grand Tour and greater ease of foreign travel, by the trading of the East India Company and other merchants, and by the voyages of explorers like Captain James Cook. These influences made themselves felt in literature, architecture, the sciences. It is easy to see what pride ordinary people took in being English, often to the point of eccentricity. There was almost no sympathy from the man in the street for the explosion of popular revolution across the Channel in France. Dr. Johnson, wrote Boswell, "was of the opinion that the English nation cultivated both their soil and their reason better than any other people."

Yet a price was to be paid. Very soon the England of Johnson was to become overcast with the shadow of industrial change. The families who had been drawn to the free religious atmosphere of new towns like Manchester, Birmingham, Sheffield, and Liverpool were having to contend with new problems of urban development, mass employment conditions and public health. New formulas would have to be worked out for agriculture, too, if the terrible fluctuations in the price of bread were to be contained. If violent revolution in the cotton-mills and coal-mines was to be avoided, Radicalism would have to make its voice heard, and find its representatives. It is easy to look back on the period and criticize contemporaries for not being better prepared for the new age, but no one could anticipate the dizzying speed at which changes would occur. Wordsworth wrote:

> Beneath the Hills, along the flowery vales,
> The generations are prepared; the pangs,
> The internal pangs are ready; the dread strife
> Of poor humanity's afflicted will,
> Struggling in vain with ruthless destiny.

APPENDIX
The Cost of Living

Here is a miscellany of facts and figures gathered from contemporary sources:

INCOMES

Firemen were paid 6*d*. each for a small chimney fire, 1*s*. for a larger one, 2*s*. 6*d*. for a building on fire (£15 payments were made to widows after a fire in Old Palace Yard, London, when firemen were burned to death)

Income of the Bishop of Winchester, about £5,000 a year

Income of John Wesley as a curate, £30 a year

Wages of London craftsmen, about 3*s*. a day from 1718

Wages of London workmen, about 2*s*. a day from 1735

Wages of provincial craftsmen, 1*s*. 6*d*. to 2*s*. a day

Wages of provincial workmen, 10*d*. to 1*s*. 6*d*. a day

Wages of workmen (potteries, iron, coal, etc.), 1*s*. 3*d*. to 2*s*. a day (women 6*d*. to 1*s*.; children 3*d*. to 7*d*. a week)

Salary of highly skilled Wedgwood pottery craftsman, £100 a year

Reward for catching a highwayman, £40

Reward for catching an Army deserter, £1

Annual fees of Principal Magistrate of Westminster, about £500 (Henry Fielding only took about £300)

Painting the dome of St. Paul's: in the reign of Anne, Thornhill was paid 40*s*. per square yard for this

Robert Owen in 1785, aged fifteen, was paid £25 a year plus board and lodging while working for Mr. Palmer the draper, but eventually left for £40 a year in Manchester, then a very high salary indeed

Cost of a postilion's new livery in 1757 (Bedford House), £4 16*s*. 11½*d*.

Cooks' and kitchen-maids' wages in 1750, £8 a year

Footmen's wages about 1700, £3 a year

Footmen's wages about 1770, £15 a year

COMMODITIES AND SERVICES

Imported "Crimson Genoa" velvet, 27*s*. a yard

Writing-desk made for Henry Purefoy by Mr. Belchier of St. Paul's Churchyard, London, £3 10*s*. 0*d*.

Venetian blinds, late eighteenth century, cost 1*s*. per square foot

Deal stool made by Thomas Chippendale, 1s. 3d.

"Large strong elm chopping block for the kitchen," made by Thomas Chippendale, 10s.

Insurance: a seven-year returnable deposit of 12s. for every £100 insured (Westminster Fire Office, 1717); an insurance mark or sign, individually made, to be displayed on the insured premises, 1s. 8d.

Water-supply: Bedford House paid £7 16s. 0d. yearly for water from the New River Company for water purer than the Thames

Bread, 2d. a pound (1767–70)

Cheese, 3½d. a pound (1767–70)

Meat, 3d. to 4d. a pound (1767–70)

Butter, 5½d. to 8d. a pound (1767–70)

House-rent, fires, tools, for an agricultural worker, about £3 a year

Coal, 13s. 6d. a ton in Newcastle, £2 to £4 in London

Premium paid on behalf of pauper children apprenticed to learn a trade, £3 10s. 0d.

Lavender-water bought from Richard Robinson of New Bond Street (1721) 5s. 2d. per pint

Two trout specially cooked at a Salisbury inn in 1695, 1s.

Asses' milk in 1796, 3s. 6d. a pint

Cup of coffee in a coffee-house, 1d.

To hire a newspaper, 1½d. plus deposit

Postage on a letter from London to Norwich, 3d., to Edinburgh, 7d., to America, 1s.

Cost of sending a harpsichord from Andover to London in a hay-wagon to be tuned and sent back, ten guineas

To decorate and furnish David Garrick's new house in the Adelphi, London, £1,000

ENTERTAINMENT AND TRAVEL

Cost of Society of Artists (Royal Academy) exhibition catalogue in 1759, 6d.

Cost of a year's subscription to Covent Garden Theatre in 1742, twenty guineas

Private concerts: music for a ball at Bedford House in 1759, fourteen guineas, to pay the musicians (three violas, one hautboy, a pipe and tabor and two basses). A French horn player who brought his own instrument was paid three guineas.

Convivial clubs: an evening's entertainment and drinking, 1s.

Admission to Vauxhall Pleasure Gardens, 1s.

Admission to cricket match between Middlesex and Essex, 1790, 6d.; prize money 200 guineas

From Strand to Westminster by boat, 6d.; Strand to Chiswick, 2s. 6d. return

London hackney-coachmen had to pay £59 for twenty-one years' licence, plus an annual tax of £4, or 10s. a year after 1711. Fixed fare was 1s. a mile

Bibliography

CONTEMPORARY WRITERS

Boswell, James, *The Life of Johnson* (1791)
Burney, Fanny, *The Early Diary of Fanny Burney 1768–78*, edited by
  A. R. Ellis
Campbell, R., *The London Tradesman* (1747)
Defoe, Daniel, *Tour through the Whole Island of Great Britain* (1724–7)
Eden, Sir F. M., *The State of the Poor* (1797)
Fielding, Henry, *Tom Jones* (1749)
——, *Amelia* (1751)
The Gentleman's Magazine
Goldsmith, Oliver, *The Vicar of Wakefield* (1766)
——, *The Deserted Village* (1770)
Moritz, C. P., *Journeys of a German in England* (1782)
The Purefoy Letters 1735–81, edited by G. Eland
Saussure, César de, *A Foreign View of England in the Reigns of George I and II*
Tucker, Dean Josiah, *Instructions for Travelers* (1757)
Woodforde, Rev. James, *Diary of a Country Parson 1758–81*
Young, Arthur, *A Six Weeks Tour through the Southern Counties* (1768)

GENERAL WORKS

Ashton, T. S., *An Economic History of England*
Besant, Sir Walter, *London in the Eighteenth Century*
George, M. Dorothy, *London Life in the Eighteenth Century*
Plumb, J. H., *England in the Eighteenth Century*
Turberville, A. S. (ed.), *Johnson's England*, two volumes
Watson, J. Steven, *The Reign of George III*
Williams, Basil, *The Whig Supremacy*

Picture Credits

The Author and Publishers wish to thank the following for permission to reproduce the illustrations on the pages mentioned: the Trustees of the City Art Gallery, Bristol, page 40; the Trustees of the British Museum, pages 8, 14, 15, 27, 51, 93, 100 and 105; the Courtauld Institute of Art, page 77; Messrs. J. R. Freeman and Co., pages 8, 14, 15, 16, 34, 35, 37, 38, 39, 51, 58, 59, 64, 82, 84, 106 and 120; the National Maritime Museum, Greenwich, pages 105 and 109; the Trustees of the National Portrait Gallery, pages 2, 18, 25, 30, 43, 68, 77, 101, 112 and 118; the Trustees of the Victoria and Albert Museum, the jacket picture; the Weaver-Smith Collection, pages 10, 22, 23, 24, 28, 50, 56, 76, 84, 110, 113, 117 and 121. All the remaining illustrations are the property of the Wayland Picture Library.

Index